Norma Vally's

KITCHEN FIX-UPS

Bonus
DVD
Included

Norma Vally's

KITCHEN FIX-UPS

More Than 30 Projects for Every Skill Level

WILEY

Wiley Publishing, Inc.

For general information on our other products and services or to obtain technical support please contact our Customer Care Department within the U.S. at (800) 762-2974, outside the U.S. at (317) 572-3993 or fax (317) 572-4002.

Wiley also publishes its books in a variety of electronic formats. Some content that appears in print may not be available in electronic books. For more information about Wiley products, please visit our web site at www.wiley.com.

Library of Congress Cataloging-in-Publication Data:
Vally, Norma.
  [Kitchen fix-ups]
  Norma Vally's kitchen fix-ups : more than 30 projects for every skill level.
    p. cm.
  ISBN-13: 978-0-470-25157-7
  ISBN-10: 0-470-25157-3
  1. Kitchens—Remodeling—Amateurs' manuals. 2. Kitchens--Maintenance and repair—Amateurs' manuals. 3. Do-it-yourself work. 4. Women construction workers. I. Title. II. Title: Kitchen fix-ups.

TH4816.3.K58V35 2009
643'.3—dc22

                                    2008046693

Printed in the United States of America

10 9 8 7 6 5 4 3 2 1

Book production by Wiley Publishing, Inc., Composition Services

credits

Acquisitions Editor
Pamela Mourouzis

Project Editor
Donna Wright

Editorial Manager
Christina Stambaugh

Publisher
Cindy Kitchel

Vice President and Executive Publisher
Kathy Nebenhaus

Interior Design
Tai Blanche

Project Photography
Matt Bowen

Illustrations
Karl Brandt
Ronda David-Burroughs
Brooke Graczyk
Shane Johnson

A mother is a person who seeing there are only four pieces of pie for five people, promptly announces she never did care for pie.

—Tenneva Jordan

Funny how, as a teen, I remember thinking, Oh God, never let me be like my mother—only to find myself as an adult praying that I could possess but a fraction of her grace and selflessness. I know, without question, I am who I am because of her love, patience, nurturing, perpetual support and unyielding faith in me. Her spirit is so bright it can light a stadium. How blessed am I to have been raised by a mother like this!

I think back to the hours Mom and I spent talking, laughing, crying, singing, dancing, eating, and of course cooking, all in the kitchen. What lovely serendipity that now, in this book focused on kitchens, the very room where she fed my soul and filled my heart, I can formally dedicate every page, every word, to her—my beautiful mother.

Mama, with each manicotti shell we've filled together, each time you've refilled my plate when I wasn't looking, each moment you filled my world with your tenderness and care, I say thank you, thank you, thank you!

A little girl, asked where her home was, replied, "where mother is."

—Keith L. Brooks

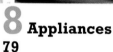

acknowledgments

Writing these books reminds me of the proverb "It takes a village to raise a child." I've often referred to these books as my babies, and *raising* them certainly would not have been possible without the help of so many wonderful people. To the exceptional staff of Wiley Publishing, especially Cindy Kitchel, Pam Mourouzis, and Donna Wright, and to Jason Marcuson and Jim Lightle at its onset—sincere thanks for your efforts and vision in creating this series. To my literary agent, Maura Teitelbaum, thank you for your continued support. For all of the technical assistance, tremendous thanks to Dave "The Heart" Carpenter, Bill "Stemmie" Harper (Big Daddy's Plumbing Repair Parts), Joe Barry (Ray Barry & Sons), Alfredo Anelli, and especially my cousin Sal Pino. Much thanks to Le Gourmet Kitchen—Bruce Colluci, Jonathan Salmon, and Jamie Gaudio (Silly Girl).

Huge appreciation to my beautiful family, especially Mama Grace, Brother Berto and Janne, Aunt Rose-Marie, and The Medinas. To all of my incredible friends, especially Lucia, Phyllis, Maria, Jordan, Aldo, JD, Barbara, and The Neils—thank you for putting up with my whining! Special thanks to Rick Medina for this series' inception and unceasing work and belief in me and our vision. Additional thanks to Eric McCullough, Michael Rhodes (The Home Depot), Ben Kunkel (Porter Paints), Cory Mennell (The Tile Shop), Eric Town (Fernco), Todd Kuhnert (Moen), Mitch Zoch (Eljer), Brasscraft, Neoperl, and especially the team at Ryobi.

Additional Photography

top left, p. 6: ©Ben Fink
top right, p. 6: ©iStockphoto.com/David Newton
bottom, p. 6: ©iStockphoto.com/Lorraine Kourafas
top, p. 7: ©iStockphoto.com/Guy Sargent
bottom, p. 7: ©iStockphoto.com/Slobo Mitic
p. 14–15: ©iStockphoto.com/Terry J. Alcorn
p. 54–55: ©iStockphoto.com/Dmitry Kutlayev
p. 102–103: ©iStockphoto.com/Leslie Banks
p. 172–173: ©iStockphoto.com/Guy Sargent
p. 186: ©iStockphoto.com/Melanie DeFazio
p. 199: ©iStockphoto.com/Keith Binns

a note from Norma

Paris, circa 1989, I'm on stage singing with a rock and roll band in the hottest night club at the time, *Les Bain Douches,* when Prince, that's right *Prince,* comes out on stage to do a song with the band. I nearly dropped dead.

How I got from that stage to swinging a hammer, TV shows, and books on home improvement? I have no idea . . . it would probably take years on a therapist's couch and a whole other book series to explain that one.

Here's what I do know, feeling helpless is never fun, especially in your own home. Something as simple as not knowing what to do as you watch your toilet bowl overflow onto the floor can be traumatizing. Without the know-how, means, or even opportunity of finding a qualified and trustworthy professional to manage a project will leave you feeling frustrated, exhausted . . . helpless.

When I started working construction in Brooklyn with my cousin Sal *umpteen* years ago, every job I walked in on, the initial reaction was always the same—they'd mumble behind my back, *What's she doing here?* They never thought I was a worker. *Is that his girlfriend? Is she here to take a coffee order? She must be the designer.* When I'd start hauling in sheetrock, strapping on a toolbelt, and getting to work heads turned, eyebrows raised, and the questions shifted to, "How did you learn how to do all this stuff?" My stock response, "Well it ain't brain surgery!"

Recognizing homeowners' feeling of helplessness motivated me to reach out and say to them, "Hey, if I can do this, so can you." I'm so grateful that I've been able to build various platforms that provide me with a means to get this message out there in an entertaining and empowering way.

I hope this book will give you the inspiration and information you need to make your kitchen the well-functioning and delightful space you want it to be.

I've often said, you can take the girl out of Brooklyn, but you can't take the Brooklyn out of the girl. So in closing, let me leave you with a Brooklyn-spirited motto that I've come up with—words I think we can all live by—Go Fix, YOURSELF!

Thank you!

Live happy,

Norma Vally

Introduction

In the neighborhood where I live when I'm in Brooklyn (and where I used to live in France), it's commonplace to shop at a specific store for a particular product. You go to the bakery for bread, the fish market for clams, the butcher for lamb shank, the candy shop for jelly rings, and so on. While it's not the quick one-stop-shop you get from supermarkets or club stores, it's the only real way to get that authentic, freshly prepared, hard to find, imported or domestic, mouthwatering good stuff. You can feel it the moment you walk into that particular shop, take a sniff, and know exactly why you're in there—oh, the semolina bread just came out of the oven. I'll take four loaves, please!

In this series of books, I sought to bring that specialty shop intensity to the reader. This book is jampacked with detailed projects and topics as they relate to a particular part of your home. I believe that total submersion is the most powerful way to excite, educate, and enrich a do-it-yourselfer. Blanket topic books certainly have their place, as do the mega-marts of America, but when you want to get into the nitty-gritty, down and dirty of a particular space in your home, this is the series to dive into.

About This Book

Have you ever noticed that no matter how big a home is, everyone still congregates in the kitchen? It's so odd that folks would squeeze themselves into the hottest room of the house when there's a lovely living room with big cushy couches just steps away. What would instigate such behavior? For me, the answer is clear: The kitchen is the heart of the home. We're drawn to the thump of the heartbeat, the lifeline, or, more literally, simmering sauces and clanging pots.

Growing up an Italian American, the kitchen was not only the heart but the brain, lungs, and every other major organ that pumps life into a space. I can't remember a discussion, argument, or celebration that didn't take place over a bowl of pasta and a glass of wine. Clearly, there's something about the kitchen that goes well beyond filling our bellies. Kitchen life fills our souls—and that's why it's the most important room of a home.

Kitchen projects and makeovers are usually the most costly and complicated of any room in the home. Look, it's as easy as one-two-three doesn't typically relate to home improvement projects, especially to kitchens. I actually resent how loosely the expression is used in the home improvement realm. Granted, some projects are easier than others, but often obstacles come up in the simplest of projects, making one-two-three more like one through sixty-four. I paid careful attention to inform the reader about all the pertinent scenarios that may arise when working on a particular project, even what you should consider before getting started.

I enjoyed conveying information in a way that's fun, clear, and approachable. Be it through labeled illustrations or shooting-from-the-hip straight talk, I animated the projects so the reader can be comfortable with them. Even more, I literally bring projects to life with the enclosed DVD that highlights particular how-to's—I'm doing them, right there in front of you, step by step. The projects are identified with a DVD icon in the book.

Another standout aspect of this book is that it truly contains projects for everyone. Whether you're a novice or an aficionado, projects range from simple to advanced as they pertain to each aspect of the room, making this book a comprehensive resource for any skill level.

How This Book Is Organized

The first three parts address projects that increase in degree of difficulty—simple to moderate to advanced—with the last part stepping outside how-to and into design. Each project includes a "Consider This" section. I provide these points so you can fully wrap your brain around pertinent aspects of each project—from drying times to potential complications and warnings. Before getting started on the core project, I present a "Prep Work" section because prep work is sometimes the most important part of a project.

While compiling projects for this book, it struck me that home improvement projects remind me of treatments on a spa menu. A telltale sign of a spa junkie, I'll admit, but isn't it true that "makeovers" relate to homes as well as to people? So I ask, do you want a quick rejuvenating makeover or an intensive overhaul? Is it simply the countertop that needs refreshing, or do you need to install a new counter? Hence, these chapters are broken down as though they were selections from a spa menu, where in this case, your home gets the treatment and you, my dear reader, are the cosmetologist.

■ PART 1: EXPRESS FACELIFT

This section offers quick, easy, and inexpensive how-to projects. If you don't have the time, skill level, or budget, you can still make refreshing fixes to your kitchen that will improve its looks as well as the quality of your kitchen life. A total beginner will thrive in this section.

Between cooking, splattering, spilling, and eating, the kitchen sees a lot of action, which, of course, translates into a lot of wear and tear. A loose faucet, stained countertop, faulty dishwasher—all these issues need to be corrected in order for your kitchen to maintain a happy and well-operating environment. In this section, we'll explore the basic maintenance, repairs, and refurbishes that will keep your kitchen running well and looking fresh.

■ PART 2: CORRECTIVE TREATMENT

This section tackles projects that go deeper than the surface. Here, you'll make repairs at a level that requires moderate investments of time and money but gives big impact. If you consider yourself "kind of handy," these projects will be a breeze.

More than any room in the house, the kitchen requires corrective treatment, especially if it's a working kitchen—one that's not just for show like in some homes where the only real wear and tear is on the trash can being overloaded with takeout containers, paper plates, and beer bottles. (Remind you of any bachelors you know?)

Real working kitchens—ones where preparing meals, serving families, baking, and holding gatherings actually occur—will eventually need to be fixed, both functionally and aesthetically. Whether it's repairing the food disposal or tiling a backsplash, in this section we tackle projects that are vital in keeping your kitchen up to speed with the demands you place on it.

■ PART 3: INTENSIVE TREATMENT

This section tackles larger, more complex tasks. Although we're not tearing out rooms and changing footprints, we are going after projects that require a more advanced skill level than a novice do-it-yourselfer has.

I'm very excited about this section. Here's a place where we can really roll up our sleeves and dig into meaty projects. Their complexity requires and assumes a working knowledge of all basic construction aspects: plumbing, electric, carpentry, and masonry.

Know that, while I've tried to account for many of the different scenarios and challenges that may occur with a project (so you're not left in the lurch saying "Hey, wait a minute, that's not in the book!"), it's impossible to predict and cover them all. Let me say through experience, *expect* to hit roadblocks here and there; they just come with the home improvement territory.

I always encourage DIYers to step out of their comfort zone and tackle bigger and bigger projects, although not without first being fully aware of the safety aspects and ramifications that accompany them. As they say, the best defense is a good offense, so do your DIY homework. Read through the entire project first, paying careful attention to all the points in the Consider This section. Then get out there and have yourself a fixin' good time!

PART 4: TOTAL INDULGENCE: DREAMING UP THE PERFECT KITCHEN

Using this section, you can knock down all barriers of entry for you to be able to dream up your perfect kitchen. Speaking of knocking down, I'll explore changing the layout, or even the footprint, of your kitchen—projects typically best left to remodeling professionals. I'll guide you into discovering what's best for you and your family's kitchen lifestyle.

When you read this section, put the do-it-yourself aspect and budget aside. Let the sky be the limit! Fully indulge your senses and discover all the innovative and exciting materials, trends, and designs that are available for kitchens today. I encourage dreaming big and exploring all options so when you take those first steps to professionally remodeling your kitchen, you'll know what *going big* can really mean.

Mama always told me to reach for the stars—the worst thing that can happen is you'll land on the moon . . . or a bamboo countertop, in this case.

Part 1

Express
Facelift

Sinks

A clog, low water pressure—a nonfunctioning sink can practically shut down a kitchen. It's good to know that minor repairs can get your sink up and running in no time.

Faucet Aerator Maintenance

WHAT YOU'LL NEED

Tongue-and-groove pliers (with taped jaws so as not to mar the faucet finish)

Penetrating oil*

Old toothbrush

* If applicable

Is the water flow at your faucet so low that it takes 10 minutes to rinse one dish? The lack of pressurized flow is probably due to a clogged aerator. The *aerator* is a small filtering device at the tip of your faucet. It contains one or more screens that serve two functions—filtering out particles and creating a smooth, neat flow of water.

Over time, these screens become clogged, which causes the water to lose pressure as it flows out of the faucet. The particles clogging the screens may also cause the spout to sputter. Simply cleaning the screens will get that full flow going again.

CONSIDER THIS

- Whenever you take something apart, be sure to remember what order the parts go in. In this instance, place the aerator parts down one at a time and in order from left to right, as if you're creating an exploded view of the aerator and all its parts. Then work in reverse when putting it back together.

- Some aerators are flush within a wider nozzle, making them less obvious to locate and remove. Look for flat ridges on the aerator where you'll grip the pliers.

- You may find various types of aerators to replace your existing one that offer special features like an on/off lever and directional sprayer. Low-flow replacement aerators are also a great choice to reduce water consumption (see the "High-Efficiency Aerators" sidebar on page 18).

PREP WORK

- Close the drain so you don't lose any parts.

- If the faucet is old or you see mineral deposits around the aerator, spray the aerator with penetrating oil and let it soak in for about 15 minutes to make the unscrewing easier.

1 With the pliers, unscrew the aerator.

2 Brush out the screen with an old toothbrush. Depending on the aerator you have, there may be more than one screen with accompanying rings. Carefully pull them apart and brush out the particles.

3 Run the water without the aerator in place. You may be surprised at what comes out and how the water goes chug-a-lug without the aerator in place.

4 Reassemble the aerator and screw it back to the faucet. Snug it tight with the pliers.

High-Efficiency Aerators

Rinsing dishes, filling containers, running the food disposal, scrubbing pans—the kitchen faucet is one of the most frequently used fixtures in a house. So why not use an aerator that can reduce water consumption, conserve energy, and help save money on your water bill, all without jeopardizing "rinsability"?

High-efficiency aerators are low flow (they use fewer gallons per minute than standard aerators), but because of their design, they provide steady, powerful pressure. Some, like the Neoperl, are also designed to resist lime buildup, which will obstruct your stream. If you regularly fill the sink to wash dishes or fill large pots for cooking, look for an aerator that enables you to flip between high- and low-flow functions when speed is an issue.

When choosing a high-efficiency aerator, look for water-saving certifications like the Environmental Protection Agency (EPA) WaterSense label, and then verify that the fit is compatible with your faucet type.

Tighten a Loose Faucet

WHAT YOU'LL NEED

Basin wrench or tongue-and-groove pliers

Installation tool*

Penetrating oil*

Flashlight

Old pillow or blanket

Rubber washers*

* If applicable

Aggressive wear and tear on a kitchen faucet can cause the faucet to loosen and end up wiggling around the sink or countertop. This problem must be corrected to prevent future damage to the faucet and to stop water from dripping under it and into your cabinet. What's happening is that the nuts of the faucet under the sink have loosened and are no longer securing it snugly to the sink or countertop. Snugging this connection back down is a quick-and-easy fix.

CONSIDER THIS

To keep your faucet from loosening in the future, it's important not to jar or tug on the handles or spout—as when kids use the spout like a grab handle to help hoist themselves up high enough to reach the sink. Aggressive wear and tear may lead to a more serious problem that won't be easily fixed with a simple project like this one.

PREP WORK

- Working under a sink is always cramped and awkward. To make more room for yourself, remove all your under-the-sink articles. (How do we accumulate so much stuff?)

- Put down an old pillow or blanket to lie on so you can be more comfortable as you work.

- Stand a lit flashlight under the sink for better visibility.

- If the nuts seem corroded and unmovable, spray them with penetrating oil and let them soak.

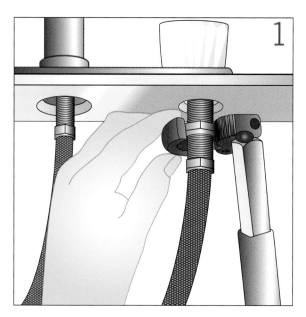

THE PROJECT

1 Examine the locking nuts under your faucet. With your pliers or basin wrench, tighten the nuts under the faucet until they're snug.

2 If the nuts have bottomed out, add a couple of rubber washers to each nut. This will add more depth to enable the nut to grab against the sink and pull down the faucet. To do so, first shut off the water at the shut-off valves, unscrew the supply lines with tongue-and-groove pliers, and then unscrew the nuts. Now you can add a couple of rubber washers inside the nuts. **Note:** Some faucets have a mounting nut(s) or plate that may be tightened where no supply line needs to be removed. Also certain faucets come with a special installation tool that is used to tighten this nut or plate.

3 Screw everything back into place, being careful not to overtighten.

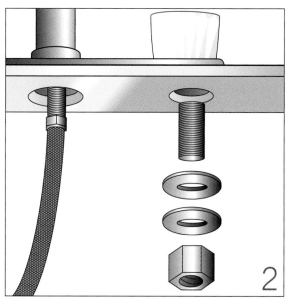

Unclog a Drain

WHAT YOU'LL NEED

Classic-style plunger (not the flanged type for toilets)

Petroleum jelly

Gloves and safety glasses*

* If applicable

Kitchen sink clogs are practically a given with all the food and grease that find their way down the drain (especially around the holidays when a clog is the *last* thing you need). Plunging a clog clear is highly effective when done properly. Follow these little tricks and save yourself a call to the plumber—and a ruined dinner party.

CONSIDER THIS

- When your sink first shows signs of a slow drain, try pouring boiling water down it to break up the formation of a clog.
- The best way to avoid clogs is not to let food debris—especially coffee grounds and grease—go down the drain to begin with.
- If you've already poured a chemical drain cleaner down the sink, you must wear eye protection and gloves in case there is splashing when plunging.

PREP WORK

- Make sure the sink has enough water in it so that the rubber of the plunger is submerged under water.
- Apply a bead of petroleum jelly around the rubber ring of the plunger to help create a better seal (a).

THE PROJECT

1 At an angle, place the plunger over the drain. Try to prevent air from being trapped in the plunger. Remember that water, not air, will force the clog down.

2 Thrust the plunger up and down about 20 times, always maintaining a seal.

3 On the last plunge, thrust the plunger up in one forceful motion.

4 Repeat if necessary. Add water if the rubber is no longer submerged in water.

5 Once the drain is clear, run hot water down it to clear any remaining debris.

A Word on Chemical Drain Cleaners

Chemical drain cleaners sound like the quick-and-easy solution to a clog—just pour it and forget it, right? Wrong. These products are extremely corrosive and can damage pipes as well as the user if not handled properly.

When poured in a standing clog, the product can sit at the bottom of a pipe and actually eat through it instead of the clog. Then, if the chemical fails to break through the clog and snaking is necessary, you run the risk of splashing these harsh chemicals everywhere while trying to clear the blockage.

Consider using an enzymatic drain cleaner that uses biological forms of chemical reactions to "metabolize" and clear the clog. These cleaners do take longer to respond to a clog, but they're noncorrosive, making them safer for you, your pipes, and the environment.

If you do choose to use a chemical drain cleaner, follow these safety tips:

- Never look down over the drain during or after pouring in a chemical drain cleaner—it can give off toxic fumes and actually erupt.
- Never mix chemical products—a chemical reaction could cause boiling and splattering.
- Choose the right cleaner for the specific clog—for example, some products work better on grease as opposed to hair.
- Always wear safety glasses and gloves, and work in a ventilated area.
- Always follow all the manufacturer's safety precautions.

Fix a Sprayer

WHAT YOU'LL NEED

Toothbrush
White vinegar
Small container for soaking
Replacement washer/rings*

* If applicable

When a sprayer leaks or loses its ability to spray, it's usually due to mineral deposits that build up around the nozzle and/or washers and rings. A good soak and brushing makes for an easy fix.

CONSIDER THIS

If you're having difficulty pulling out the sprayer, check the hose under the cabinet. It's probably getting tangled around some plumbing or under-the-sink paraphernalia.

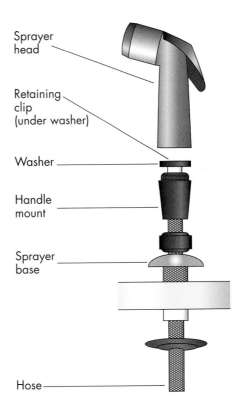

Sprayer head

Retaining clip (under washer)

Washer

Handle mount

Sprayer base

Hose

THE PROJECT

1 Unscrew the sprayer from the hose.

2 Brush the nozzle with vinegar. If there is a lot of buildup, soak it in vinegar. Be careful not to let it soak for too long, because this may mar the finish.

3 Run water through the sprayer to clear out any debris.

4 Inspect any washers or rings. (Remember in what order you remove them.) Soak and scrub these if there's buildup. These parts may need to be replaced if they're highly corroded.

5 Screw back the sprayer, turn on the water, and check for leaks.

Countertops

Simple repairs can refresh the entire look of your countertop. Tile repairs can even restore your counter's ability to ward off bacteria growth. Be it aesthetic or hygienic, check out these quick fixes.

Restore a Solid-Surface Countertop

WHAT YOU'LL NEED

Mild liquid abrasive cleanser

Rag

Sponge

Towel

Abrasive pad kit for countertops or pack of sandpaper ranging from fine to superfine

Polish and protector product (designed for your countertop material)

Scratches and stains on a countertop can make your entire kitchen look worn out. Happily, solid surface countertops (synthetic sheets formed by polyester and/or acrylic resins) allow you to buff away most unsightly marks; blemishes are easily sanded away.

CONSIDER THIS

- The most common cause of staining is water sitting on the counter surface. Always wipe your countertops dry.

- Use cleaners and polishes that are designed for your countertop material and that are suitable for food-handling surfaces.

- The manufacturer of your countertop may sell specially designed powders, sprays, or creams that aid in removing blemishes and return it to its original finish.

PREP WORK

- Using a sponge or rag, clean the countertop with a mild liquid abrasive cleanser. In a circular motion, work through all surface residue.

- Wipe down the countertop with water and dry it with a towel.

- Examine the remaining stains and scratches and determine which pad in the kit is abrasive enough to work through them. There's no need to abrade much deeper than the blemishes. With a little "test" scratch, choose a pad that creates a slightly deeper abrasion than your existing blemish.

THE PROJECT

1 With the proper grit pad, sand back and forth over the scratches/ stain, going slightly beyond the damaged section (in order to blend with the rest of the surface). Then switch directions, so the motion goes from north–south sanding to east–west. Wet the area with water slightly as you're working.

2 Repeat Step 1 with the next finer grit pad.

3 Continue to buff out the blemishes, moving to finer and finer pads until the desired finish is achieved.

4 Finish by applying a polish and protector suitable for your surface. Check with your countertop manufacturer for the proper product.

Is butcher block a stumbling block?

If your countertop is all or part butcher block, you may be frustrated by the darkening and scratches that have built up over time. You can renew the surface by sanding with progressively finer-grit sandpaper (see the instructions on this page), but be sure to sand in the direction of the grain.

For darkening, try a half-water/half-chlorine bleach solution or use a wood bleach, following the manufacturer's instructions.

Once the surface is blemish free, rub in a beeswax or mineral oil that is suitable for food-preparation surfaces to help seal and restore the wood's natural luster.

Replace a Cracked Tile

WHAT YOU'LL NEED

Replacement tile

Masonry cold chisel or dull wood chisel

Nail set and hammer

Drill/driver

¼-inch masonry drill bit

Grout saw

Scraper

Notched trowel

Grout tile float

Small pry bar*

Putty knife*

Safety glasses

Gloves

Rags

Tile adhesive

Matching premixed or powdered grout

Mixing pail and stir stick (for powdered grout)

Large man-made tile sponge

Bucket

Grout sealer

*If applicable

Cracked tile on a countertop is more than unsightly and dangerous (because of a sharp edge)—it can harbor bacteria inside the crack that can make your countertop less than sanitary.

CONSIDER THIS

Be careful! Tile shards are very sharp. Wear gloves and safety glasses.

PREP WORK

- Remove the tile by scraping out the grout joints with a grout saw (a).

- Punch small divots in a big X across the face of the tile with the nail set and hammer. With the divots as starting points, drill holes through the tile (but *not* through the substrate of the counter) to weaken it and create a break point (b). Now break out the tile in small pieces with the hammer and chisel (c and d).

- Once the tile is out, scrape away any remaining adhesive. Use the grout saw to clean the edges of the adjoining tiles.

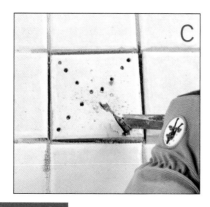

THE PROJECT

1 Spread tile adhesive on the back of the tile using the short end of the trowel or scraper. Run grooves through the adhesive. Do the same to the counter space.

2 Insert the tile in the space and gently press it in place using the butt of your fist. Check that the tile is sitting flush with the others. Be sure that the grout lines are even and lined up with the existing ones. Wipe away any adhesive that may have squeezed out onto the surface.

3 Allow it to dry overnight.

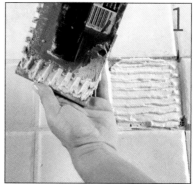

4 To fill in the grout lines, use a grout float to press the grout into the joints of the tile lines. It's best to hold the float at an angle and pass over the area firmly in a diagonal direction.

5 With a damp sponge, gently wipe away the grout that remains on the face of the tile.

6 As the grout dries, a powdery residue will form. Gently wipe it away with a soft, clean rag, being careful not to wipe out any of the grout.

7 Apply grout sealer following the manufacturer's instructions.

Appliances

Nothing can continue to operate without some basic maintenance. When we neglect things, we end up with bigger issues that often result in headaches and costly repair bills—like my root canal (that could have totally been avoided had I not let a cavity grow into the size of a punch bowl). Appliances should rank on the top of your maintenance list and become a routine part of your do-it-yourself life.

Dishwasher Maintenance

WHAT YOU'LL NEED

Replacement spray arm (contact the manufacturer or an appliance center for the proper replacement)*

White vinegar

Scrub brush

Pipe cleaners

* If applicable

Common issues, like a clogged spray arm or leaky door, are easily managed with the following fixes.

THE PROJECT: Cleaning the spray arm

If the spray arm becomes clogged or cracked, water won't disperse properly, which will make for dirty dishes.

1 Shut off the electricity to the dishwasher from the power source.

2 Remove the lower dish rack and examine the spray arm. (Now is also a good time to clean the food trap.)

3 There should be a screw that holds the spray arm in place. Unscrew it—likely turning *clockwise*. (Note that while *lefty-loosey, righty-tighty* is a good general rule, spinning parts are often reverse threaded, meaning *righty loosey*.) If there's no screw, rock the arm back and forth while pulling it up and out.

4 Soak the arm in white vinegar and water. Scrub the holes with a brush and clean them with pipe cleaners. Rinse water through it.

5 If the spray arm is cracked, it will need to be replaced.

WHAT YOU'LL NEED

Replacement gasket (contact the manufacturer or an appliance center for the proper replacement)*

Pliers

Flathead screwdriver

Proper type and size driver (as needed, if applicable)

Hot soapy water

* If applicable

THE PROJECT: Fixing a door leak

If you find a little puddle at the base of the dishwasher, first try to identify where the water is coming from.

CONSIDER THIS

- **Check that it's not coming from one of the hoses.** Shut off the electricity to the dishwasher from the power source, and remove the bottom cover plates. Inspect for any loose hose connections and tighten if necessary (a).

- **Check that the door closes tightly.** When the door is locked closed, give it a jiggle. If there's play, it needs to be tightened. There should be a latch that can be adjusted with a screwdriver. Turn it in small increments, and test how it closes—it should be snug, but not overly tight, causing you to force or bend the latch (b).

- **Examine the *gasket* (the rubber strip that runs around the door).** If it's cracked, torn, or brittle, it will need to be replaced.

1 Shut off the electricity to the dishwasher from the power source.

2 Soak the gasket replacement in hot, soapy water—this will make it more pliable and easier to install.

3 Open the door and remove the bottom dish rack.

4 Examine the gasket to see how it's attached. There may be retaining screws or tabs holding it in place, or it may simply be wedged in its track. Loosen the tabs or screws. Use pliers or a screwdriver to pry or slide out the gasket.

5 Press or slide the new gasket in place. If there are tabs or screws, fasten them as you go.

Basic Dishwasher Tips and Maintenance

- Regularly remove any debris that has accumulated on the strainer or anywhere in the dishwasher.
- Repair any cracked or missing plastic coating on the dish racks with a vinyl touch-up paint made specifically for dishwasher racks. Worn racks with exposed metal can corrode and rust, which will eventually get rust on your dishes and flatware.
- If your dishwasher sits unused for over a week or has developed a musty smell, pour in a cup of white vinegar and run it on a light cycle.
- To boost hot water, run the hot water at your sink until it's good and hot, and then start the dishwasher.
- If you have a food disposal, always run it to clean out any stagnant debris before starting a dishwasher load.

Refrigerator Maintenance

WHAT YOU'LL NEED

Replacement gasket (contact the manufacturer or an appliance center for the proper replacement)

Pliers

Flathead screwdriver

Proper type and size driver*

Hot, soapy water

Household detergent

Mineral oil*

* If applicable

Correcting a faulty door seal and other regular maintenance will keep your refrigerator in tip-top shape.

THE PROJECT: Fixing a door with a faulty seal

CONSIDER THIS

If your door doesn't give you that "tug" when you go to open it, you have a faulty seal. That tight seal is what keeps the cold air in and warm air out. An improperly sealed door will cause the condenser to run excessively—wasting energy and money and ultimately causing the unit to wear out before its time.

- **Test for an improperly sealing door by placing a business card on the door jamb and closing the door.** If, when you try to pull it out, there's no resistance at all, you have a faulty seal.

- **Check to see whether the door needs to be realigned or the hinges need to be tightened.** Hinges may be hidden under caps. Pry them off and check that the screws are snug. If the door sags, loosen the screws, realign the door, and then retighten the screws.

- **Check that the fridge is level.** A tilt could impair its ability to close and function properly. Check for level by placing a level on top of the unit. Adjust the leveling feet as needed by screwing them higher or lower.

- **Examine the *gasket* (the rubber strip that runs around the door).** If it's cracked, torn, or brittle, it will need to be replaced.

1 Turn off the refrigerator and remove any food from the door.

2 Soak the gasket replacement in hot, soapy water—this will make it more pliable and easier to install.

3 Pull out the old gasket. Gaskets are secured in various ways: Screws, clips, springs, a retaining strip, or glue may be used. Typically, you pull back the old gasket to reveal the retaining screws. Loosen the retaining screws (but don't unscrew them completely) in order to release the gasket. Observe and remember how the gasket lip fits into its channel.

4 Clean any debris that may have accumulated under the gasket with a household detergent.

5 To install the new gasket, set it around the door and begin working it into place, smoothing it down as you go. Don't tighten any screws yet.

6 Once the gasket is in place, barely snug the retaining screws, starting from the top and working your way down. As you go, test the door for warping by opening and closing it; loosened retaining screw can make some doors very flexible. If there's warping, finesse the door by pushing and pulling the top and bottom of the door to straighten it out. Once it's straight, finish tightening down the screws.

7 If there's drag or squeaking from the gasket, rub some mineral oil along the gasket on the hinged side of the door. It may take several days for the gasket to be properly formed.

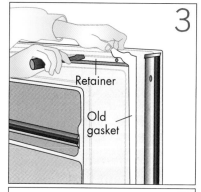

Basic Refrigerator Tips and Maintenance

* Vacuum condenser coils about twice a year—if you have pets that shed, once every few months. Dust-laden coils are taxing to the unit and make it run less efficiently. The coils are found on the back of the unit or beneath it, behind a grille. Typically the grille can easily be pried off by hand. Turn the refrigerator off and then use a vacuum attachment to reach the entire length of the coil.
* Refrigerators with drip pans need to be emptied and cleaned a few times a year. Remove the bottom grille and, with a flashlight, locate the pan. Slide it out, wash, rinse, and replace. Wear gloves— mold and slimy residue may have accumulated in the pan.
* Regularly wash the gaskets and door jambs with a household detergent. Debris along these surfaces will eventually create faulty seals.

Stove Maintenance

Burners repairs and other basic maintenance will keep the heat on and you cookin', good lookin'.

> **THE PROJECT: Replacing an electric burner (element) that won't heat**

Often, one stinker of a burner, for no apparent reason, just stops heating up. Meanwhile, the other three are just fine. Why? Troubleshooting that question is the key to this fix.

PREP WORK

- First, unplug the stove.

- Test the nonfunctioning burner in a working receptacle (socket). Most burners simply pull out from the socket with a lift and a jiggle (a). Some sockets require you to remove a screw to release the burner (b). If the burner doesn't work in a functioning socket, it needs to be replaced.

- Next, test whether a functioning burner works in that receptacle. If it does, there's probably a minor connection issue with the nonfunctioning burner. Scrubbing the terminals with a wire brush and spreading them out for a tighter fit should do the trick.

- If a functioning burner does not work in that receptacle, the socket will need to be replaced.

a

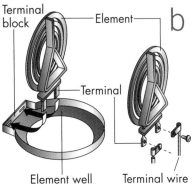

Terminal block — Element — b

Terminal

Element well   Terminal wire

1 Locate the clip and/or screw that secures the damaged socket and detach it from the range.

2 Unscrew the wires that are attached to the socket.

3 Connect the wires to the new socket and attach it to the range following the reverse steps performed to detach it.

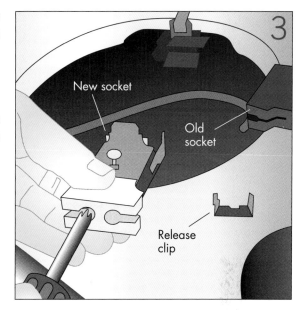

New socket

Old socket

Release clip

Appliance Touch-Up Paint

A nasty nick on your appliance can be a real eyesore. Happily, touch-up paints can easily cover most nicks and scratches. When choosing a paint, see if your appliance manufacturer offers one for your unit in order to achieve a perfect color match. Make sure you choose one that is formulated for high temperatures if touching up an oven or range.

For best results:

- Sand the blemish with fine sandpaper and then wipe it clean with mineral spirits.
- Use the provided applicator brush or a small artist's brush to apply the paint.
- Let it dry completely according to the manufacturer's recommended drying time.
- To fill in deep nicks, repeat these steps by building up thin layers, always being sure that the paint dries thoroughly, and then lightly sanding between coats.

WHAT YOU'LL NEED

Toothbrush

Large sewing needle

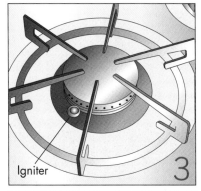

Burners that won't ignite are most often caused by food spills that block gas and ignition pathways. A good cleaning is usually all that's needed to get those puppies to fire up again.

1 The gas to the range does not need to be turned off, but make sure the burner knobs are in the off position.

2 Remove the burner grates and lift up the hinged cooktop. (Sealed burners don't have this feature but can be cleaned from the top.)

3 Locate the pilot hole or igniter—it will be located between two burners. (On sealed burners, there will be a small nub on the burner itself.)

4 Brush the debris from these locations (a) and poke clear any holes with the needle (b).

5 Remove and clean the burner cap.

6 Brush and poke clear all holes on the burner itself.

Basic Stove Tips and Maintenance

- Regular cleaning with a household degreaser around gas or electric burners and drip pans will help avoid future ignition/heating issues. Wipe spills while they're still warm (not hot—be careful not to burn yourself!)—cold, dried spills that become caked on are harder to clean and more damaging to ports and connections.
- Regularly clean the grease screen(s) in the range hood for more efficient exhaust. Remove them, and then spray and/or soak them in a household degreaser. Make sure they're completely dry before reinstalling them in the hood.
- Never spray cleaners directly into any control panel on your unit—spray them into a paper towel or cloth, and then wipe the surface.

Cabinets

Cabinets can be magnets for grease, scratches, and fingerprints. They can also look passé with dated hardware, knobs, and pulls. An express facelift is just what you need to make your cupboards go from scruffy to spiffy.

Add or Replace Knobs and Pulls

WHAT YOU'LL NEED

New pulls and/or knobs with screws

Phillips screwdriver (or proper type and size of driver depending on screws)

Drill

Appropriately sized drill bit (to be determined by the diameter of the knob/pull screw)

Drawer pull jig

Center punch

Washers*

Tape measure

Pencil

Newspaper

Penetrating oil*

Safety glasses

* If applicable

It's amazing what a small piece of hardware can do to change the look of your entire kitchen. You can set a mood, look, and theme with these little guys—a lot of power packed into something whose literal purpose is simply to open and close doors and drawers. Talk about *bang for your buck!* Maybe that's why some knobs and pulls can be priced upwards of $25 . . . each!

CONSIDER THIS

- If your cabinets already have knobs/ pulls and you want to use the existing holes, be sure to bring the old hardware with you for proper fit. The length and diameter of the screw of the hardware can vary, as can the spread between screws.

- If you're unhappy with the existing knob/pull placement, you can fill the holes. Use wood dowels, smooth over with wood putty, sand, and then finish with touch-up paint. Obviously, the success of your results will be in how well you're able to match the finish. Another option is to use an escutcheon or wide-based knobs/pulls if your new placement is close enough to the old holes and can be concealed by the new ones.

- If your cabinets have no knobs/pulls, you'll need to decide where to place them. With drawers, it's pretty much a given—dead center. But with doors there's no set rule. The best way to decide is to hold the knob/pull up to the door and temporarily stick it in place so you can step back and take a look. Use a reusable adhesive like DAP Bluestik.

- It's worth investing in a drawer pull jig for consistent hole placement when doing several cabinets. This tool is a marking template that you set to your hole specification. With it, you can quickly and easily get accurate results without having to remeasure each and every door/drawer.

  Measure the depth of the door/drawer where the screw will go to be sure that the knob/pull you choose is the right length and comes with the proper-length screws. If the screws are too long or too short, you can purchase different ones—just be sure that they're the right diameter to fit the knob/pull.

PREP WORK

- Clear away articles from the countertop and in the drawers.

- Put newspaper beneath the cabinets to catch sawdust.

- If your cabinets have existing knobs/pulls, remove them by unscrewing them from their screws. Use a little penetrating oil if they're stubborn.

THE PROJECT

Two things are crucial when adding knobs/pulls: that your hole placement is perfectly consistent on each door/drawer and that you drill your holes straight through the material, not on an angle. For consistent hole placement, we'll be setting up a jig made specifically for this purpose. As for driving the bit straight, keep your eye on the drill relative to the cabinet/drawer so that the bit is constantly at a right angle to the surface.

1 With a pencil and tape measure, mark the center of each drawer or the desired height for the pull on the door edge.

2 Line up the drawer pull jig to your desired hole location(s). Place it on the top of the drawer or door edge, line up the center marks, and then mark the corresponding holes of the template onto the cabinet surface with a center punch.

3 Wearing safety glasses, carefully drill the holes, being sure to drive the bit straight through the material. Be sure to steady the door so it doesn't move as you're drilling. Start drilling slowly with steady pressure.

4 Clear away any sawdust.

5 Insert the screw through the hole from the back of the drawer/ door, and then place the knob/pull over the tip of it. Get the screw started by hand, and then tighten it with a screwdriver. If the screw is slightly too long and won't snug against the door/drawer surface, you can add a washer.

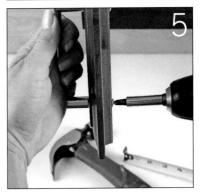

Restore Wood Cabinet Finish

WHAT YOU'LL NEED

Proper screwdriver for knobs/pulls

Mild detergent*

Newspaper or tarp

Bucket

Scrubbing sponges

Soft, clean rags

Penetrating oil*

Murphy Oil Soap

Old English Scratch Cover (in light or dark according to your cabinet finish)*

Howard's Restor-A-Finish

Howard's Feed-N-Wax

* If applicable

The steps you take to revive your cabinets' finish will be determined by asking yourself one major question: How bad are they?

If they have minor scratches, grease buildup, and discoloration, restoring them is as simple as various steps of cleaning and polishing. Keep in mind that this process restores an *existing finish*.

If they are deeply blemished and/or have a severely flaking surface, the fix upgrades to a refinishing process, which involves stripping and reapplying a *new finish*—certainly doable, but definitely more involved (see "Refinish Wood Cabinets" on page 87).

PREP WORK

- Remove all objects from the countertop.
- Spread newspaper or a tarp beneath the cabinets.
- Remove the knobs/pulls by unscrewing them from behind with a screwdriver (a). Store them in a safe place. Use penetrating oil on the screw head if they're stubborn. Now's a good time to give them a thorough washing with detergent if they're stained or sticky (b). A good soak in hot water and mild detergent will help.

THE PROJECT

1 Give the cabinets a good initial washing with Murphy Oil Soap—follow the manufacturer's instructions on dilution. Allow the cabinets to dry and take a look. This may have done the trick. Are there still *minor* scratches? Use Old English Scratch Cover in light or dark, and rub it over the entire surface of the cabinet.

2 If, after the initial cleaning, you still see substantial blemishes, use Howard's Restor-A-Finish to blend scratches and remove stains. This product goes on with a cloth in a wipe-on, wipe-off process. Follow the manufacturer's instructions. (This product cannot be used on polyurethane finishes. Always test a product like this one in an inconspicuous area first to see how it reacts to your wood finish.)

3 Give the cabinets a final coat of Howard's Feed-N-Wax to buff and protect the finish. The manufacturer recommends that this product be applied and left on for about 20 minutes and then buffed off.

4 Fasten the knobs/pulls back to the doors and drawers when they are thoroughly dry.

Can I paint my wood or Formica cabinets?

You bet you can! If the existing finish is severely scratched and flaking, it will need to be stripped first (see "Refinish Wood Cabinets" on page 87). However, if the cabinet surfaces are stable with minor blemishes, the process is pretty straightforward.

Proper preparation of the surfaces is crucial for professional-looking results. First, remove hardware, doors, and drawers. Wash all the surfaces with nonammonia-based detergent. Then sand the surfaces to create a "tooth" for the paint to stick to. Once sanded, wash and wipe them down so they're dust free. You should be left with a clean, dull, dry surface before applying paint.

Prime and paint the surfaces with compatible high-quality products. After priming, let dry and then lightly sand before painting. My experience is that oil-based paints dry harder and are more durable than latex. Oil paints give off fumes, so work in a ventilated area and follow manufacturer's safety instructions. Cut in with a brush and then use a ¼-inch-nap roller for large surfaces. Smooth down any orange-peel marks or streaks from the roller with a brush. The key is to apply *thin* coats, allowing each coat to dry and then lightly sanding with 400-grit sandpaper before applying the next coat.

Spraying on paint with a pneumatic sprayer is what the pros do—but it's really an art. Sagging and dripping, not to mention overspray and fumes, can become quite the challenge.

Walls and Floors

Projects from this section remind me of what a good shampoo, conditioning, and haircut can do for the way you look. Like our hair, walls and floors need basic care to keep them looking, and even performing, their best. Which reminds me, I have to make an appointment to do my roots, get a trim . . . .

Patch Holes in Drywall

WHAT YOU'LL NEED

4-inch putty knife
Utility knife
Newspaper or old towel
Nylon mesh tape
Spackle
Fine sandpaper

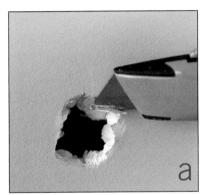

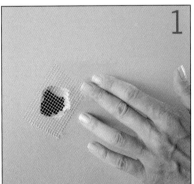

Swiss cheese isn't only found in the cold-cut drawer of your refrigerator. Your kitchen walls can start to look like Swiss cheese from all of the holes left after removing cabinets or repositioning a spice rack or cork board. Here's how to patch various sized drywall holes.

THE PROJECT: Patching small holes (1–3 inches)

PREP WORK

- Put down newspaper or an old towel to protect the floor beneath the hole.
- With the utility knife, cut out any bits of drywall that are protruding out of the hole (a).
- Lightly scuff up the painted area around the hole with the sandpaper (about an inch around).

1 Place a piece of nylon mesh tape over the hole. For very small holes (like from a screw and plastic anchor), this step is not necessary.

2 With a dab of spackle on your putty knife, smear the spackle over the hole and tape.

3 Smooth out the spackle, and let it dry. If when it's dry you see that another coat is needed, sand lightly and pass another coat.

4 When it's completely dry, sand any raised edges, prime, and paint.

WHAT YOU'LL NEED

4-inch putty knife
Level
Speed square
Utility knife
Drywall saw
Plaster trowel
Newspaper or old towel
Pencil
Tape measure
Scrap piece of drywall
Joint compound (or mud)
Fine sandpaper

THE PROJECT: Patching medium holes (4–6 inches)

PREP WORK

- Put down newspaper or an old towel to protect the floor beneath the hole.

- With a level to mark straight lines (a), cut out a clean square around the hole with a drywall saw (b). Lightly scuff up the painted area around the square with the sandpaper (about an inch around).

- Take the measurements of the square opening, add 2 inches to each side, and then trace and cut a scrap piece of drywall to those dimensions.

This patch has many names—hot patch, hat patch, and blow patch are some of them.

1 Place your square drywall patch face down and, with a speed square, trace out the dimension of the square hole.

2 Score the lines with a utility knife, and then bend and crack the drywall rock. Now peel the rock off the paper. Do this to each side. You'll be left with what looks like a square hat that has a 2-inch brim.

3 Test to see that the patch fits snugly in the hole. Adjust if necessary.

4 With a putty knife, smear a generous layer of joint compound all around each side of the hole.

5 Press the patch into the hole and smooth the brim down with the putty knife.

6 As the joint compound squeezes out from behind the brim, spread it over the entire surface of the patch.

7 With the trowel, pass more joint compound over the entire surface of the patch. Let it dry.

8 Sand any raised edges and pass another coat, being sure to feather out the edges. You may need to repeat this step.

9 When it's completely dry, sand smooth, prime, and paint.

WHAT YOU'LL NEED

Drywall saw

Drill/driver

Speed square

Utility knife

4-inch putty knife

Plaster trowel

Newspaper or old towel

Level

Pencil

Tape measure

Scrap square of drywall
(match the thickness of your wall—usually ½ inch)

Two-by-four length(s) of wood

1⅝-inch drywall screws

Joint compound

Fine sandpaper

THE PROJECT: Patching large holes (smaller than 8 inches)

PREP WORK

- Put down newspaper or an old towel to protect the floor beneath the hole.

- With a level to mark straight lines, cut out a clean square around the hole with a drywall saw. Lightly scuff up the painted area around the square with the sandpaper (about an inch around).

- Take the measurements of the square opening, and then trace and cut a scrap piece of drywall to those dimensions (cut on the inside of the pencil line so the square is slightly smaller than the hole). Now you have your patch square.

- Cut a length of two-by-four, 4 inches longer than the hole.

1 Insert the first two-by-four into the hole. Line up the flat side of the two-by-four on one side of the opening.

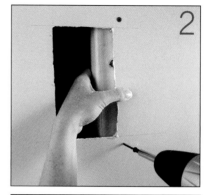

2 Secure the two-by-four to the wall by driving a screw into the two-by-four above and below the hole. **Note:** For a smaller hole (6–8 inches), one two-by-four centered in the opening will suffice. Drive a screw halfway in the middle of the two-by-four to use as a handle so that it doesn't drop behind the drywall as you're screwing it in place.

3 Secure the two-by-four to the other side of the opening in the same manner.

4 Insert the patch square into the hole and screw it to the two-by-four with a couple of screws on each side.

5 Put nylon mesh tape over each joint (a). With a putty knife, smear joint compound over each seam (b). Let it dry.

6 Sand any raised edges and pass another coat of joint compound over the entire patch, being sure to feather out the edges. Once it's dry, repeat this step for your final coat.

7 When it's completely dry, sand smooth, prime, and paint.

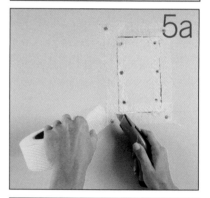

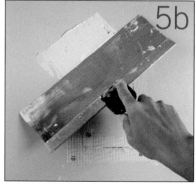

Repair Torn Vinyl Flooring

WHAT YOU'LL NEED

Matching scrap flooring

Straightedge (a framing square or metal level)

Utility knife

Notched trowel

Masking tape

Vinyl floor adhesive

Wax paper

A few heavy books

Liquid seam sealer

Moving a heavy appliance, like a refrigerator or stove, can be a real pain—and not just in the back. The weight of them can easily put a tear right through your vinyl flooring. I've seen it happen so many times—yep, did it myself when I pulled out my fridge to vacuum the condenser coils. Ugh! The good news is that if you have a matching scrap piece, you can make that tear virtually disappear.

CONSIDER THIS

You'll need a piece of matching scrap. If you don't have one left over from the installation, see if you can obtain some scrap from the store where you purchased the flooring. If you can't find a scrap, you can cut out a piece from beneath the refrigerator or stove—just don't tear the floor again when trying to get to it.

THE PROJECT

1 Take a piece of scrap flooring, place it over the tear, and center it so that it covers one entire flooring pattern. Make sure that the scrap piece is large enough to cover one whole pattern plus a couple of inches extra around each side.

2 With the replacement piece lined up, tape it to the floor.

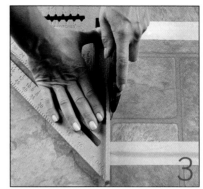

3 Using a straightedge and sharp utility knife, cut out the full pattern, slicing through both the scrap and the existing flooring. It'll take a few passes.

4 Remove the tape and scrap (which is now cut to the identical patch size).

5 Peel up the old damaged section with a putty knife.

6 Scrape away any adhesive left on the subfloor.

7 Dry-fit the cut replacement patch—fine-tune if necessary with a utility knife. Bevel the backside of the edges to help it lie in seamlessly.

8 Apply adhesive to space with a notched trowel, let it get tacky, and then position and drop in the patch, pressing it in place.

9 Wipe the joints of any adhesive that may have oozed out.

10 Place a piece of wax paper over the patch and weigh it down overnight with some heavy books.

11 The next day, apply a liquid seam sealer, following manufacturer's instructions.

Replace a Damaged Vinyl Tile

Replacing an entire damaged tile section is simple because no patch cutting or pattern matching is necessary. Simply heat up the damaged tile with a blow dryer (to soften the glue), and then scrape/pry up the old tile and any glue residue left on the subfloor with a putty knife and scraper. Trowel on floor adhesive, let it get tacky, and then lay in the replacement tile. If you have the peel-and-stick type of tile, just peel and stick!

Reseal a Damaged Wood-Floor Section

WHAT YOU'LL NEED

Vacuum or broom

Nonresidue wood cleaner

Mop

Fine-grit sandpaper

Tack cloth

Wood sealer or stain and sealer
(compatible with your floor's finish)

Rags

Mineral spirits*

* If applicable

Wood floors are likely to get worn in patches around high-traffic areas, like in front of the fridge. Resealing these sections and performing regular maintenance on the entire floor will keep it sound and refreshed for many years (see the sidebar "Basic Floor Tips and Maintenance" on page 53).

CONSIDER THIS

A simple water-drop test will reveal the condition of your wood finish. Drop a bit of water on the floor—if it beads up, it's sound. If it spreads out and absorbs or discolors the wood, it's time to reseal the finish. If the worn areas are not limited to small spots here and there, the entire floor will probably need to be refinished, see "Refinish Wood Floors" on page 96.

THE PROJECT

1 Clean the floor thoroughly with a nonresidue wood cleaner. (Don't use products like Murphy Oil Soap.)

2 Make sure the floor is completely debris free and dry before continuing.

3 Lightly sand the affected area, being sure to feather the edges so there are no overlap marks. If staining has occurred, try to remove the stain with more vigorous sanding in that spot, but again, feather the edges.

4 Vacuum the sanded area (a). Then wipe up all dust with a tack cloth (b).

5 Apply the sealer. Some sealers are in a touch-up spray form, like Dura Seal Touch-Up Spray. Others are brushed or mopped on. Follow the manufacturer's instructions. You may need a stain/sealer if the stain has been worn away.

6 Be sure to wipe up any excess sealer, especially where the old finish is still present. Sometimes a second coat may be necessary.

Basic Floor Tips and Maintenance

Wood floors. Warm and charming, easy on the feet—you gotta love a beautiful wood floor. They do, however, require some special TLC.

- Vacuum (sweep) and damp-mop floors frequently, especially if you have pets. Debris on the floor acts as sandpaper, so when you walk on it, it'll prematurely wear away the floor's finish.
- Clean up spills right away.
- Regularly use a cleaner/protector specially formulated for your floor's finish.
- Put felt or plastic glide pads on your furniture legs to prevent scratches.
- Don't use furniture polish on your floor—it'll create an extremely slippery surface.
- Use rugs in high-traffic areas, like in front of the sink or fridge.
- Conceal scratches with a tinted wax stick or small amount of furniture scratch cover.

Tile and natural stone floors. Durability and beauty are the obvious assets to tile and stone floors. But let's not forget: Although they are low maintenance, they're *not* maintenance free. Unsealed grout, chips in ceramic, a worn granite finish—these types of distress will make any tile or stone floor look shot and shabby. Here are some tips for maintaining tile and natural stone floors:

- Vacuum (sweep) and damp-mop floors frequently, especially if you have pets. Debris on the floor acts as sandpaper, so when you walk on it, it'll prematurely wear away the floor's finish.
- Clean up spills right away.
- Regularly use a cleaner/protector specially formulated for your floor's surface. Cleaners should have a nonoil, nonanimal-fat base.
- Put felt or plastic glide pads on your furniture legs to prevent scratches.
- Reseal grout every year or so, or when cracking and chipping begin to occur.
- Reseal stone when water drops no longer bead on the surface.
- Repair chips in ceramic tile with ceramic touch-up paint.

Part 2

Corrective
Treatment

Sinks

Whether it's the *drip-drop* of a leaky faucet, or dead silence of one that won't drain, you could *drip-drop* dead from the hefty repair bill a plumber will slap on you for his house call. Often all you need is $20 cartridge replacement, or whirl of a $15 plumber's snake to get your faucet and sink fixed. Oh, what a relief! Now that's a good reason to collapse.

Repair a Leaky Faucet

WHAT YOU'LL NEED

The following tools should be on hand for any of the following faucet-type fixes.

Flathead and Phillips screwdrivers

Needle-nose pliers

Adjustable wrench

Tongue-and-groove pliers

Allen wrenches (hex key)

Cartridge puller (for cartridge type only)

Valve-seat wrench or seat dresser tool (for compression type only)

Clean rag

Metal nail file

Masking tape

Penetrating oil

Heat-resistant plumber's grease

Steel wool or scouring sponge

Flashlight

Repair kit: washers, O-rings, cartridges, discs, and so on (depending on your type of faucet)

Plastic bags

When looking to fix that annoying and wasteful *plip-plip* from the kitchen faucet, the first thing you must do is identify which type of faucet it is from an internal standpoint. In general, there are four faucet types: *compression, ball, cartridge,* and *disc.* These names actually depict the part that controls the water flow.

You can make an educated guess as to which type your faucet is based on characteristics I mention in this section, or you can contact the manufacturer directly. Being the adventurous type, I like to just open up the faucet (which you'd have to do anyway) and take a look around. It makes me feel like a doctor doing exploratory surgery. When you think about it, with what plumbers charge, the medical and plumbing fields have a lot in common.

CONSIDER THIS

You must locate and check that your faucet shut-off valves are working properly before starting this project. These faucet repairs require that you shut the water off from the water supply shut-off valve. These shut-offs are usually located under the sink—one for the hot and one for the cold. If you ever want to experience an *I Love Lucy* calamity firsthand, unscrew the faucet handle and start to dismantle the parts without shutting the water off from the valve. Water will start shooting out into your face like a geyser.

Once the water is off at the shut-off valve, slightly turn on the faucet to verify that it's completely off and to release the pressure.

Note that your faucet may vary slightly from what is described and illustrated.

Keep track of the order in which parts are disassembled to help you when you're putting them back together.

PREP WORK

These steps apply to all the following faucet fixes:

- Shut off the water to the faucet from the shut-off valves. This step is imperative to avoid a flood.

- Close the stopper and lay a rag in the sink so nothing falls down the drain and it's protected.

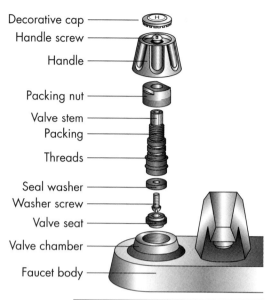

Decorative cap
Handle screw
Handle
Packing nut
Valve stem
Packing
Threads
Seal washer
Washer screw
Valve seat
Valve chamber
Faucet body

THE PROJECT: Compression-type faucet

The compression-type faucet is the oldest, most common, and least expensive of the four. Compression-type faucets always have two control handles. A stem with an affixed washer raises and lowers, which opens and closes the water valve as you turn each handle. What usually goes bad on this type of faucet is the washer or valve seat that gets worn out from the compression and grinding.

Know that you may have a choice on how to proceed with this fix. You can either repair the old valve assembly or replace it with a new replacement cartridge—many manufacturers are now offering this as an option. Check online or with your plumbing-supply store about a replacement cartridge for your compression-type faucet. If the cartridge is available, go with it! Although it will be more expensive initially, it'll last much longer than seats and washers. Just follow Steps 1–3 and Step 5 (skip Step 4), and then insert the cartridge.

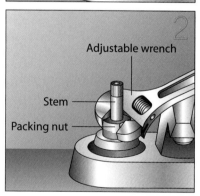

1 With the water shut off from the shut-off valves, remove the handles. To do this, you must locate a screw that's usually hidden beneath a decorative cap. Gently pry the cap off with a metal nail file or flathead screwdriver. With the screw exposed, unscrew it and lift off the handle.

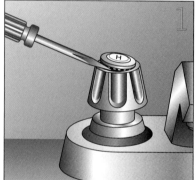

Adjustable wrench

Stem

Packing nut

2 Locate the packing or retaining nut. With tongue-and-groove pliers or an adjustable wrench, turning counterclockwise, unscrew the packing nut, and put it to the side.

3 With the valve stem now exposed, pop the handle back on the stem, and use it to easily unscrew the valve assembly up and out of the valve chamber.

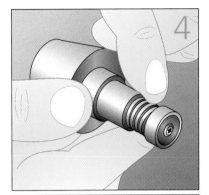

4 On the bottom of the valve stem, you'll see that the washer is screwed in place by a single brass screw. It'll likely be split and corroded. It may have even broken off and be sitting in the valve chamber. It's best to take the entire assembly to the plumbing store for the correct washer replacement.

5 In addition to installing new washers, you should examine the valve seat. Run your finger along it to see if there are bumps that would prevent a tight seal (a). If there are imperfections, you must correct them either by replacing or by redressing the valve seat—which will depend on the type of seat you have.

- A replaceable valve seat has a hex or slotted shape in its center. You'll need a *valve-seat wrench* (b) to unscrew it. Insert the wrench and unscrew the valve seat. Bring it to the store for replacement.
- A fixed-type valve seat has a simple round hole in it. You'll need a *seat-dresser tool* (c) to resurface the seat. Insert the seat dresser into the chamber and give it a few spins to "dress" the seat. Do so until the seat looks shiny. Be sure to wipe away the metal shavings with a rag once it's dressed.

6 With steel wool or a scrubber, clean the valve stem.

7 Screw on the new washer, being sure that it's snug, but not deformed.

8 Hand-screw the valve stem back into the chamber, and then reinstall the retaining nut with pliers or a wrench.

9 Pop the handles back on, but don't screw them on yet. Turn the water back on and make sure nothing is leaking. Screw on the handles, snap on the caps, and you're done!

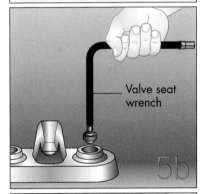

Valve seat wrench

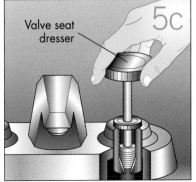

Valve seat dresser

THE PROJECT: Ball-type faucet

A ball-type faucet always has a single control handle. A hollow metal or plastic ball rotates as you turn the handle that controls the mixture and volume of the hot and cold water. It has many little parts and, for this reason, more opportunities for leaks.

1 With the water shut off from the shut-off valves, remove the handle. Locate the set screw in the handle housing. It's sometimes hidden behind a small decorative cover. Pry off the cover with a flathead screwdriver or metal nail file, loosen the set screw with an Allen wrench, and lift off the handle.

2 If the leak is coming from the bottom of the handle, you may just need to tighten the locking collar (the adjusting collar). Use the spanner wrench that is included in the ball-type repair kit to tighten the collar by turning it clockwise. To test if this has done the trick, turn on the water from the shut-off valve and see if the leak is gone. If it is, you're done! Just screw the handle back on. If not, you'll need to disassemble the rest of the faucet.

3 Shut off the water at the shut-off valve to continue. Loosen the collar with the spanner wrench. Now remove the domed cap: First, wrap the jaws of the pliers with masking tape to protect the finish on the cap, and then twist and pull off the domed cap.

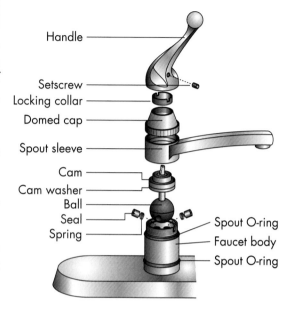

Handle
Setscrew
Locking collar
Domed cap
Spout sleeve
Cam
Cam washer
Ball
Seal
Spring
Spout O-ring
Faucet body
Spout O-ring

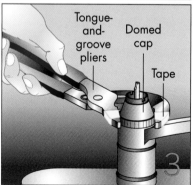

Spanner wrench
Locking collar

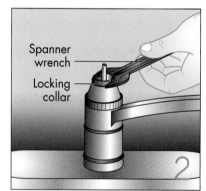

Tongue-and-groove pliers
Domed cap
Tape

4 Lift out the cam and the cam washer, and then lift out the ball by its stem.

5 Your best bet is to replace all these parts because you have the faucet apart anyway—the kit should have everything you need. Use penetrating oil around all the threads and parts to clean them off before replacing and reassembling the parts.

6 With needle-nose pliers or a screwdriver, pull out the valve seats and springs from inside the faucet. Be aware that these little parts will try to get away from you.

7 Slip the new seats and springs onto the tip of a screwdriver and drop them down into position—tap them in place with your finger. Note that the springs go in first, followed by the cupped side of the seats, which fit over the springs.

8 If the faucet is leaking at the base, it's probably the O-rings that need replacing. Pull off the spout with your masking-taped pliers and examine the O-rings. Pry them off with the hooked end of the spanner wrench or screwdriver. Put plumber's grease around the new O-rings and roll them back in place.

9 Reassemble all the parts. Insert the new ball, cam washer, and cam. Make sure that any tab and notch line up with one another.

10 Slip on the domed cap and tighten the collar with the spanner wrench. Screw on the handle and pop in the decorative cover.

11 Turn on the water from the shut-off valve and check for leaks. Nice job!

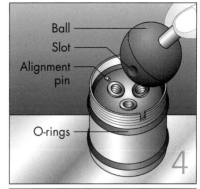

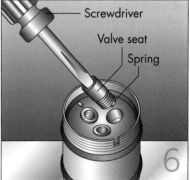

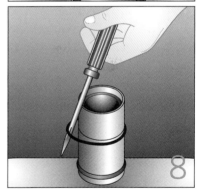

THE PROJECT: Cartridge-type faucet

A cartridge-type faucet (my favorite) uses a plastic or brass cartridge that houses a stem that slides up and down in the handle to control the water flow. This type of faucet is used in single- or double-handled faucets. It's the simplest of all types to work on because the entire cartridge slips in and out for easy repair or replacement.

1 With the water shut off from the shut-off valves, remove the handle(s). To do this, you must locate a screw that is usually hidden beneath a decorative cap. Gently pry off the cap with a metal nail file or flathead screwdriver. With the screw exposed, unscrew it and lift off the handle.

2 With the handle off, there may be a sleeve, locking nut, and/or retaining clip(s) that need to be removed. Use a wrench or pliers to remove the sleeve or nut. Use a flathead screwdriver or needle-nose pliers to remove the clip. (Faucets vary, so you may need to work through a bit of a puzzle to remove the cap, handle, nut, clip(s), and so on—be patient!)

3 Pull out the cartridge using pliers, but first look to see if there's a mark, flat side, or notch and mentally note its orientation. Pulling out the cartridge may take some patience—wiggle it out little by little. If the cartridge won't budge, see the sidebar "Using a Cartridge Puller" on page 64.

4 Examine the O-rings. If the cartridge doesn't show corrosion, but the O-rings look worn, simply replace the O-rings. Use a flathead screwdriver to pry them off. Put plumber's grease around the new O-rings and roll them back in place.

5 To replace the cartridge, bring the old one to the store with you for the proper replacement part. Remember to note the brand of your faucet. If you have a choice of brass or plastic, opt for brass—although it's more expensive, it'll last much longer.

6 To insert the new cartridge, first recall a mark, flat side, or notch to indicate orientation. Push the new cartridge in place with your finger. Plumber's grease may be recommended by the manufacturer.

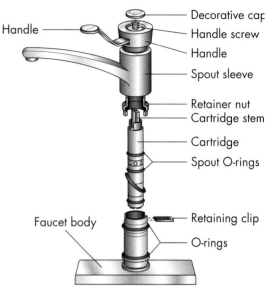

- Decorative cap
- Handle screw
- Handle
- Spout sleeve
- Retainer nut
- Cartridge stem
- Cartridge
- Spout O-rings
- Retaining clip
- O-rings

Handle

Faucet body

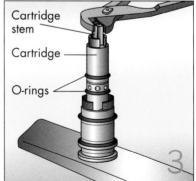

Retaining clip

2

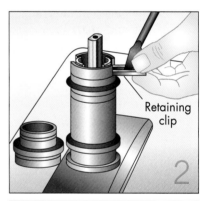

Cartridge stem

Cartridge

O-rings

3

7 Reassemble the unit—insert the retaining clip(s), locking nut, and so on (if applicable), and then reattach the handle.

8 Turn on the water from the shut-off valve and test the faucet. If it's a single-handle control, check to see that hot and cold water work in the proper handle position. If they're crossed (hot comes out of cold and vice versa), rotate the cartridge 180 degrees.

9 Replace the decorative cap. You're all done!

THE PROJECT: Disc-type faucet

A disc-type faucet is usually a single-handled control as illustrated in this project. It works like this: In a cylinder, two discs—either plastic or ceramic—glide over one another as you spin the handle. Each disc has corresponding holes that open and close as they rotate to control the flow of hot and cold water. They're practically maintenance free. But, depending on your water, seals may corrode or a disc may crack.

1 With the water shut off from the shut-off valves, remove the handle. Locate the set-screw in the handle housing. It's sometimes hidden behind a small decorative cover. Pry off the cover with a flathead screwdriver or metal nail file, loosen the set-screw with an Allen wrench, and lift off the handle.

2 Lift off the escutcheon cap, which should expose the disc assembly (also referred to as the disk cartridge or cylinder).

3 You'll probably see mounting screws. Unscrew them and lift out the cartridge—use pliers if it's being stubborn.

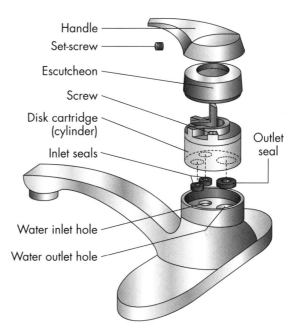

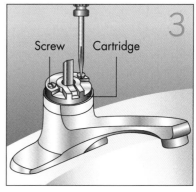

4 With the disc assembly out, you'll see three neoprene seals. Remove them (a) and clean off any debris in the recesses or on the lower disc (b) with a plastic scour pad.

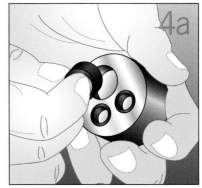

5 Insert the new seals. A cleaned disc, inlets, and new seals may be all you need to stop the leak. To check if this has done the trick, reassemble the faucet, move the handle to the on position, and *slowly* turn on the water from the shut-off valve (a sudden surge of water could crack a disc).

6 If there's still a leak, shut off the water from the shut-off valve and disassemble the faucet as described in Steps 1–4.

7 With the entire disc assembly removed, drop in a new replacement cartridge, reassemble the faucet, and screw on the handle.

8 Put the handle in the on position, and then *slowly* turn on the water from the shut-off. Give the faucet a spin and check for leaks. *Ta-da!*

Using a Cartridge Puller

When a cartridge just won't budge, which is very common with older faucets and in areas with hard water, you may need the assistance of a cartridge puller. Pullers vary according to faucet brand, so each one is set up a little differently. Be sure to find one that is compatible with your faucet type. To use the puller, you insert it into or over the cartridge by pushing or screwing the puller in place. (Typically, there is a threaded screw on the puller that screws into the old valve cartridge stem.) After the puller is engaged with the old cartridge, twist the puller slightly clockwise and counterclockwise, and then pull the cartridge straight out. This will break loose any mineral buildup and set that cartridge free.

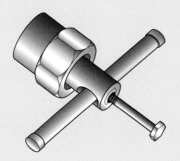

Snake a Stubborn Sink Clog

WHAT YOU'LL NEED

Tongue-and-groove pliers

Wrench

Safety glasses

Bucket

Butter knife or screwdriver

Manual crank-type plumber's snake with handle

Rags

Penetrating oil

Plunger

When plunging just isn't doing the trick, it's time to bring in the big guns. A plumber's snake or auger is a long, thin, coiled cable that literally drives through a clog to clear it. They come in varying sizes and powers—from small hand-operated ones to large motorized types used for sewer drains.

This project uses a manual crank-type snake with a handle—ideal for sinks.

CONSIDER THIS

Beware if you've already used a chemical drain cleaner on a clog. Any drain water will be contaminated from these chemicals, and attempting to snake at this point will be highly dangerous. Protect your skin, face, eyes, and nose with proper safety gear. Also, be prepared to dispose of the contaminated water from the clog promptly and carefully.

PREP WORK

- Beneath the sink, unscrew and remove the P-trap with a wrench—loosen both nuts at each end of the loop. Plastic pipes may be unscrewed by hand. Keep a bucket ready to catch the water that will now drain from the sink (a).

- Check that the P-trap is not clogged—if it is, clean it out. (The contents of this section of pipe will probably be very gross.)

- Pull the horizontal trap arm out of the *stub-out* (the short drain pipe coming from the wall).

- With an old butter knife or screwdriver, scrape clean the inside of this pipe. (It'll likely be encrusted with gunk.)

THE PROJECT

1 Insert the cable into the stub-out and keep feeding it into this pipe until it feels like you've hit the blockage.

2 Tighten the thumb screw (to lock the cable) and begin cranking the handle. It'll probably take a little force, so be prepared to steady the auger while turning.

3 Keep turning until you feel some movement.

4 As the clog breaks up, feed the cable deeper through the drain and repeat Steps 2 and 3.

5 If the cable seems to get caught on something, turn the handle counterclockwise, back out the auger a bit, and repeat Steps 2 and 3.

6 Continue these steps until the cable moves freely.

7 Turning counterclockwise, reel in the cable, close up the drain, and flush hot water down it. If it gets backed up, use a plunger at this point—it's probably due to the broken-up debris that needs to get flushed through the system. Continue flushing with hot water.

8 Before storing the auger, dry off the cable and apply some penetrating oil to prevent rust.

Countertops

A pricey new granite countertop may not be in your budget, but that doesn't mean you have to be stuck with your old one. Resurfacing your laminate countertop is an affordable way to give it an entirely new updated look—likewise with adding a new backsplash.

Resurface a Laminate Countertop

Laminate countertops have really come a long way. With so many colors, patterns, and even textures to choose from, they're an economical and good-looking countertop choice. It's fun to mix colors and patterns as well. In one of my apartments, I used two different styles—a rust leaf pattern on the bar and a speckled solid beige on the rest of the countertops. They worked together harmoniously, but at the same time created two distinctly different spaces.

What's also great about laminate countertops is that they can easily be resurfaced. If your older countertop is run-down or you want to give your kitchen a whole new look, resurfacing is an ideal choice, especially when working on a tight budget.

CONSIDER THIS

New laminate can be applied directly over your existing laminate countertop as long as the existing surface is stable. You can spot-glue small sections that have loosened along edges, but if much of the surface is loose and chipping it's best to screw down ¼-inch hardwood plywood over the entire surface in order to create a stable base for the new laminate.

Removing the old laminate is not recommended, because it often leads to damaging the substrate.

Before starting the project, allow the new laminate to stay in your kitchen for about 48 hours in order for it to acclimate to interior temperature and humidity.

PREP WORK

- Clear away everything from the countertop. Unplug and remove all appliances.

- Inspect the existing countertop. Look for sections where the laminate has pulled away from the substrate. Carefully pry open the loose section with a putty knife (being careful not to crack it) and apply the contact cement following manufacturer's instructions.

- If you're resurfacing a countertop with a sink, turn off the water at the shut-off valves, disconnect the water lines and trap, and remove the sink with the faucet still attached. (For detailed instructions on how to remove a sink, see "Install a New Drop-in Sink" on page 115).

- Sand down all the areas to be resurfaced, including any backsplash (a). This creates a tooth for the laminate to adhere to.

- Wash down all surfaces with a household detergent.

- When you're finished, the old laminate should be dry, dull, cleaned, and totally dust free.

THE PROJECT

MEASURE AND CUT

1 Take length and width measurements of your countertop.

2 First, you'll rough-cut the sheet of laminate. Using the measurements from Step 1 with an additional inch of overhang on the front and sides of the countertop, mark these measurements onto the sheet and cut them following the cutting instructions in the sidebar "How do you cut and trim plastic laminate?" on page 73.

3 Place the overcut sheet of laminate onto the countertop, fitting it tight against the wall or backsplash. Put a length of masking tape along this edge of laminate.

4 Invariably, the wall/backsplash will not be straight. Using a scribing tool, run a pencil mark onto the masking tape that will transfer any dips or bows onto the laminate for your cut line—this will allow for a perfectly snug fit.

5 Test-fit the laminate against the wall/backsplash. Sand down the edge. Wipe it clean.

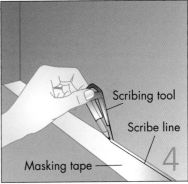

Scribing tool

Scribe line

Masking tape

GLUE THE LAMINATE

Depending on your edge trim choice, you may decide to install the trim before the top sheet. Before continuing, review "Install the Countertop Edge Trim" on the next page.

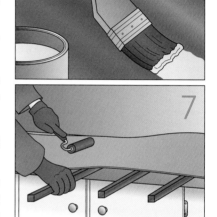

6 Lay the laminate facedown on a protected surface. Brush or roll the adhesive onto it. Then do the same to the countertop. Follow the manufacturer's setup time; this is crucial for proper bonding.

7 Place dowels or furring strips along the length of the counter every 12 inches or so.

8 Do not allow the glued surfaces to touch until they're perfectly aligned. Contact cement glues on contact, but only to another glued surface.

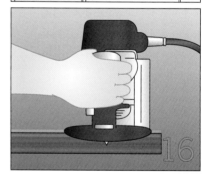

9 Place the glued laminate over the dowels and align it snug against the wall.

10 One by one, pull out the dowels, smoothing down as you go with the J-roller, until the entire sheet is glued down. Smooth down toward the edges. Continue to smooth down, especially along the edges—apply good pressure.

11 If there seems to be a bubble, put a cloth down and steam-iron it flat.

IF THERE'S AN ADJOINING CORNER OR SEAM

12 Glue down the larger piece first.

13 Follow Steps 1–8 for the second piece. Place a strip of wax paper along the seam so half of the paper is on the laminate you just glued down, and the other is on the glued countertop about to receive the new laminate.

14 Snug the adjoining piece up to the seam, and then, when tight in place, temporarily tape it down.

15 Repeat Steps 9–10. When all of the dowels have been pulled out, raise the edge of the laminate and pull out the wax paper. Roll the J-roller from the second piece toward the seam and repeat this all long the seam. Finish with Step 11.

TRIM THE EDGES

16 Once the laminate is dry, use the router to finish the edges. Rest the router base (make sure it's clean) on the countertop and slowly drive it into the edge. In a fluid motion, guide it along the entire countertop edge, being sure not to force or pause the movement. Cut the laminate flush to the counter all the way around. For further cutting instructions, see "How do you cut and trim plastic laminate?" on page 73.

IF THERE'S A SINK CUTOUT

17 The glued laminate will be covering the existing sink cutout. Looking underneath the cabinet as a reference, use a ¾-inch drill bit to cut a hole around the center of the opening.

18 With a router, insert the router bit into the hole and drive the router toward the sink edge, and then all around the opening.

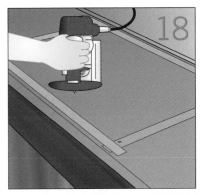

INSTALL THE COUNTERTOP EDGE TRIM

There are various materials and methods to finish a countertop edge. Consider the following options and installation steps to help make your trim choice. Keep in mind your counter shape when deciding on a trim—for example, a sweeping rounded corner will require a flexible trim.

Strips of Laminate

The most common and affordable option, strips of matching laminate are cut and glued to the counter edge. It is common for edge strips to be installed after the top sheet is glued in place, but ideally they should be installed *before* so they're covered by the top. Edge trim kits are also available by some manufacturers—these strips are usually thinner and do well with rounded corners.

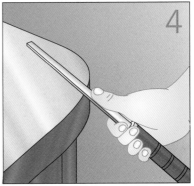

1 Measure and cut the strips (see "How do you cut and trim plastic laminate?" on page 73).

2 After gluing strips to the edge, use masking tape to hold them in place until completely dry.

3 Once they're dry, use a router to cut flush to the countertop.

4 Smooth down any rough edges with a half-round file and sandpaper.

Metal Molding

Various metal moldings are available to finish a counter edge. Brushed aluminum can give a classic 1950s soda-shop feel, while stainless can make a bold modern statement.

1 Measure and cut the lengths of molding. File the cut edges to a smooth finish.

2 After the laminate top is glued and cut flush to the substrate, glue or screw the molding in place, depending on how it's designed.

Wood Molding

Wood molding that matches your cabinets or comple-
ments the laminate is another attractive edge-treatment
option. There are various ways a wood molding can be
used to finish an edge. After the top laminate is glued
and trimmed, the most basic way to add wood trim is
to glue and then nail the molding to the substrate with
finishing nails (a). Clamp or tape the molding to the
edge until completely dry.

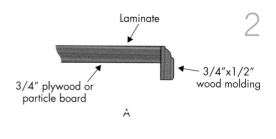

Another method of installing wood molding is to
embed it behind a strip of laminate, and then router-
cut the edge to reveal the wood (b). This method is more
intricate to execute but creates a beautiful wood inlay to
the top of the counter edge. Here's how to do it:

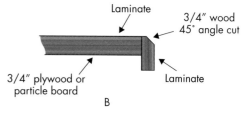

1 Glue and nail a strip of hardwood to the substrate
edge.

2 "Bury" the wood by gluing a laminate strip over it.

3 Glue down the top sheet as indicated above.

4 Choose a router bit profile (cove, ogee, round-over, and so on).
Once the wood and laminates are dry, use the router to cut into
the corner, trimming the laminates to reveal the wood.

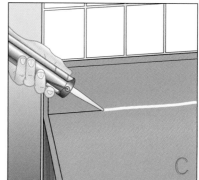

ADDRESS THE BACKSPLASH

For a backsplash, use the same cutting and gluing methods as
indicated in this section. Glue the face of the backsplash first, and
then the top. You may also install decorative wood molding to
the top of the backsplash—glue and nail with finish nails. Once
it's dry, apply a bead of silicone at the joint where it meets the
countertop (c).

How do you cut and trim plastic laminate?

While laminate can be cut with a jigsaw, handsaw, or utility knife, I find a circular saw the easiest and most efficient way to cut lengths of it.

Here are tips on how to cut laminate with a circular saw:

- Use a fine-tooth blade with the blade loaded *backward.* Because a circular saw cuts on the upstroke, you risk chipping the laminate surface. Loading the blade backward will make it cut on the down stroke, diminishing the possibility of chipping. Turning the laminate face down to cut will achieve the same results, but how do you transfer a cut line to the back of the sheet when you've marked it on the face? This especially matters when marking the laminate for a perfect fit to a wall. That's why a backward-loaded blade is a better method of cutting.
- Run masking tape along the cut line for additional chipping prevention.
- Always cut oversized to allow for trimming.

The best way to trim and flush laminate is with a router, namely a laminate trimmer. This tool is a smaller version of a wood router but specifically designed to cut laminate. It's smaller and easier to handle as well.

Here are tips on how to use a laminate trimmer:

- Choose the desired bit: Some are straight while others offer a round-over or *chamfer* (beveled) cut. Typically, the edge trim is cut straight, and the top sheet slightly beveled.
- Set the appropriate bit depth. The tool will have an adjustment device of some kind. Be sure the depth is set to cut only the laminate in question.
- Some trimmers allow you to change the base, which will offer a variety of cutting options: A straight base is fine for basic cuts while an offsetting base allows zero clearance for hard-to-reach cuts, like in a tight corner.
- To cut, rest the base on the surface, turn on the power, and then drive the bit into the material. Do not start the trimmer with the bit touching the material.
- While cutting, move the trimmer in a steady, fluid motion. Don't hesitate the bit over one section—this will cause scorching. Just keep it movin'!
- Make sure that the bit doesn't get loaded with debris as you're cutting. Clean it with a rag as you go, but be careful because it gets hot.

Always remember to unplug or remove the battery when changing or cleaning a blade or bit on any power tool.

Tile a Backsplash

WHAT YOU'LL NEED

Tiles

Tile cutter

Nippers

Notched trowel

Grout float

Putty knife

Clean rags

Large towel or tarp

Gloves

Safety glasses

Dropcloth or newspaper

Sandpaper

Tape measure

Mastic (tile adhesive)

Tile spacers

Level

Grout

Grout sealer

Large man-made tile sponge

Bucket

Waterproof caulk

Caulk gun

Clean rags

Recently, my brother, who's a bass player by profession, decided to temporarily trade in his jazz bass for a toolbelt. Among the renovation projects he took on was a tiled backsplash. I was so impressed by the job he did! I also loved how he and his wife chose a tile that complemented the floor tile and cabinets—it really pulled their kitchen together and gave it an exciting element of design.

Not only will a tiled backsplash enhance the look of your kitchen, it will also protect your walls, especially around the sink and stove.

CONSIDER THIS

Because of drying times, this project is at least a 2-day job.

The section of wall you're tiling must be free of moisture and stable. Make any wall repairs in advance of this project to allow for drying times.

You'll need to decide how high you want the backsplash to be—the minimum is typically 4 inches and the maximum is up to the bottom of the wall cabinets or range hood.

To calculate how many tiles you'll need, measure the length and width of the area for square footage—the tile box usually indicates the square footage that one box of tile will cover.

When purchasing tile, always buy extra to compensate for breakage and future replacements.

You can finish the edges with a border tile, bullnose tiles, or molding.

PREP WORK

- Clear away everything from your countertop and cover it with a protective dropcloth or newspaper.

- Shut off the power from the service panel to any outlets that run along the wall and remove their cover plates.

- Clean any residue that may have accumulated on the wall around the outlet.

- Lightly sand the entire wall to create a "tooth" for the adhesive. Wipe it down with a damp rag.

THE PROJECT

PREPARE LAYOUT FOR TILE

- If you have a tiled countertop with which you're matching the backsplash, your layout is already established—follow the existing grout lines for the wall layout.

- If you're not following an existing tile pattern, start with a full tile in one corner and dry-set a course. Now see if an unwanted sliver of tile is produced at the other end. To correct this problem, measure how much you'll need to cut from the first tile in order for the end tile to be larger. Once the cut tile sizes are established, starting from the end, mark on the wall the placement of the first whole tile. Remember to account for any border tile when measuring, if applicable.

- If you're centering a design pattern above, say, the stove, find its center, draw a plumb line on the wall at that point, and start tiling out from there (a).

- If you're tiling above a small existing backsplash, follow the appropriate scenario, as stated above, to find your starting point.

Tips on Cutting Tile

- For smaller tile jobs, a manual tile cutter (score-and-snap) is ideal. Line up the tile, then cut it by firmly passing the cutting wheel down the guide, which will score the tile. Next, press the lever that snaps the tile at the score line. It takes a bit of practice, but once you get the hang of it, it's a snap—literally.
- A small wet blade is ideal for most tile jobs. Guide the tile into the blade. Do not force it as it's cutting. Be sure there is always adequate water.
- Use a rod saw and nippers for curves and small cuts. Make the larger cuts first, and then finer cuts with these tools.

TILE THE BACKSPLASH

1 With the recommended mastic and notched trowel size, spread a layer of mastic across the bottom run of wall—but not more than will be needed for approximately six tiles.

2 At the starting point you've already established for a whole tile, press each tile in place, giving a slight twist when setting them against the wall. Press each new tile in place, making sure they sit flush with the existing tiles and with one another.

3 Use spacers underneath them, leaving enough space for a caulk bead. Likewise, use spacers in between each tile and course. Check for level as you go. Continue until all the whole tiles are in place.

4 With a putty knife, scrape away any mastic that may begin to dry as you're working. Also, with scraper, wipe away any glue that may ooze out between the tiles as you press them in place.

5 Measure, cut, and glue the tiles that need to be cut to size. Remember to always dry-fit before applying the glue. Tiles that need to be specially notched around perhaps cabinets or outlets will require extra care when cutting.

6 Glue any border tiles, if applicable. Allow 24 hours for the tiles to set before grouting.

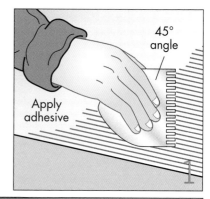

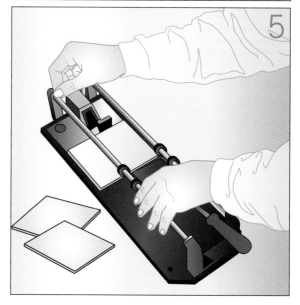

GROUT AND SEAL THE BACKSPLASH

7 To fill in grout lines, use a grout float to press the grout into the joints of the tile lines. It's best to hold the float at a 45° angle and pass over the area firmly in a diagonal direction.

8 With a damp sponge, gently wipe away the grout that remains on the face of the tile.

9 As the grout dries, a powdery residue will form. Gently wipe it away with a soft clean rag, being careful not to wipe out any of the grout. Let the grout dry overnight.

10 Apply a bead of waterproof caulk at the joint where the tile meets the counter (or at any existing backsplash).

11 After the grout is completely dry and dust free, seal the tile with a grout sealer according to the manufacturer's recommendations.

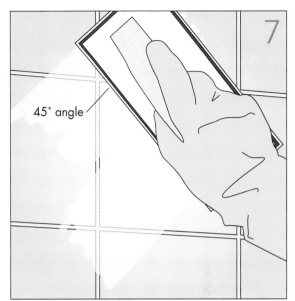

45° angle

Stainless-Steel Backsplash—Not Just for Restaurants Anymore

Stainless steel is an exciting backsplash option for do-it-yourselfers who want to instantly give an updated look to their kitchen. Normally cutting lengths of sheet metal is no easy task without the proper equipment. But by seeking out a sheet-metal fabricator that's willing to work with you, you can leave the cutting to the pros.

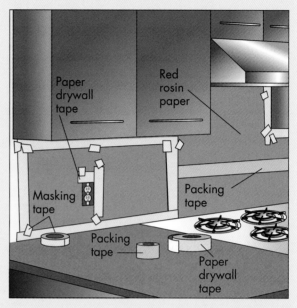

You'll need to provide the sheet-metal shop a template of the backsplash space—it's all about cutting a perfect pattern for the pro to follow. To do so, remove outlet and switch covers (shutting power at the service panel), then strategically cut and tape red rosin paper (a multipurpose paper used in construction) to the wall. With a utility knife, carefully cut out the exact shape of the wall space. You may need to piece sections together with packing tape. Use drywall tape to make precise edges where necessary. Cut out the outlet and switch openings—do not cut them too big (the "ears" of the switches and outlets will rest on the new backsplash. Bring the pattern to a sheet-metal fabricator that provides such a service.

To install, prep the wall by washing and sanding lightly. After it's clean and dry, dry-fit the template—with an exact template and cut, it will fit in perfectly. Apply a large zigzag pattern of silicone to the center of the wall and a straight bead all along the edges. Press the sheet in place and use masking tape to hold it there until the glue takes hold. Use metal caulk along the joints around the edges to finish the job.

Appliances

A food disposal that's on the blink can end up backing up your sink, which can lead to no place to rinse or wash your dishes and a sink piled up with dirty dishes. Now what? Well, a glass of scotch on the rocks would be my first choice, but alas, the icemaker isn't working either. Ugh! All kidding aside, a couple of broken appliances can really be annoying. Fix them yourself . . . then have a drink in celebration.

Repair a Garbage Disposal

We all get the urge to dump everything down the sink when we have a food disposal—and knowing better doesn't always stop us from doing so, making jams and clogs a common and annoying occurrence.

Now it would be one thing if we had a big bad Mack garbage truck under our sinks with its fierce packer blade to muscle all the waste out of sight, but, even the largest residential garbage disposal won't hold up to some of the mega wads of food scrapings and who-knows-what-else that end up down our poor little drains.

The following project addresses troubleshooting, maintenance, and repair on some common garbage disposal issues.

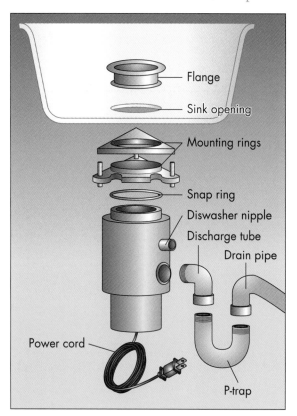

Flange

Sink opening

Mounting rings

Snap ring

Diswasher nipple

Discharge tube

Drain pipe

Power cord

P-trap

CONSIDER THIS
Warning: Always unplug your garbage disposal or, if it's hard-wired, shut off power from the service panel when working on your food disposal. *Never* put your hands down the drain into the disposal (the hopper)! Never try to unjam the unit with the power on.

PREP WORK

- Clear out everything from inside the sink and clear away everything under the sink so you can access the disposal.

- Run the cold water and quickly turn the power on and off to the disposal. If it's humming, but not turning, power is reaching the unit, but something is blocking it from spinning. If no sound is made, either the *reset button* (a device that shuts down the unit when it begins to overheat) has popped (a) or it's been tripped at the service panel.

- Shut off the power from the service power or plug.

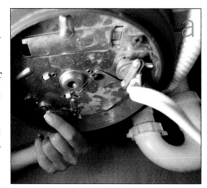

THE PROJECT

1 With the power off from the service panel or plug, look inside the grinding chamber to see if there is something visibly lodged. With long-nose pliers, try to pull it out. If it's impossibly wedged, you'll need to dislodge it by spinning the flywheel.

2 Locate the wrench hole of the flywheel that will be directly under the unit. A wrench will have been provided with the unit (if you can't find it, any store that sells disposals can provide you with one—it's often a ¼ Allen wrench). Insert the wrench into the hole and spin it in both directions until the flywheel moves freely.

3 If the disposal does not have a wrench hole, use a broom handle or large wooden spoon to push on one of the impeller arms in each direction until the jam breaks loose.

4 Look inside the grinding chamber again to pull out whatever was lodged in it. Use long-nose pliers to pull it out.

5 Return power to the disposal from the plug or service panel. Run cold water and switch the unit on. If you hear no sound, shut the unit off. Reach under the unit and feel for a reset button. If it tripped, it'll be popped out—push it back in.

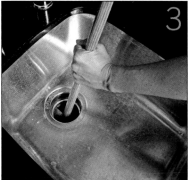

6 Run water and switch the unit on again—it should spin freely.

Basic Garbage Disposal Tips and Maintenance

If there is a leak under the cabinet from the disposal:

- Check the hoses and pipes for loose connections.
- Tighten any loose mounting bolts. If the bolts are already tight, the leak may be caused by failing plumber's putty. To reestablish the putty seal:
  - Loosen the bolts on the mounting ring and slightly lift the sink flange above the sink.
  - Scrape away the old and cracked plumber's putty (a).
  - Roll a bead of putty in the palm of your hands until it becomes long and flexible.
  - Wedge the rope of putty under the flange.
  - Tighten the bolts, which will cause excess putty to squeeze out, and wipe away the excess.
  - Retighten the bolts.
- Do not throw dense, fibrous, or stringy food—like broccoli ends or celery—down the disposal.
- Do not throw in any food that will create a paste when it's ground down, such as rice, egg shells, or coffee grounds.
- Do not wait for the hopper to be filled before running the disposal.
- Monthly, pour white vinegar and baking soda down the disposal. Once it stops foaming, flush it with running water.
- Do not use chemical drain cleaners in your food disposal.
- For a slow-draining sink, disconnect the discharge pipe from the disposal and disconnect the drain trap. Remove any debris. If the pipes are clear, the clog is farther along the drain line behind the wall—see "Snake a Stubborn Sink Clog" on page 65.

Repair an Icemaker

WHAT YOU'LL NEED

Adjustable wrenches

Screwdrivers

Multimeter (volt-ohm meter)

Small bucket

Replacement icemaker inlet valve*

Toothbrush

* If applicable

You quickly realize the value of having those little frozen cubes at your immediate disposal when the icemaker is on the fritz. You just can't instantly make ice!

There are various icemaker issues that can put the heat on your ice bliss. Some of them (like a broken thermostat) will require a professional to service, but there are minor repairs that you can certainly handle yourself.

A faulty water valve is a likely culprit when your cubes are small or hollow—indicating that not enough water is getting to the icemaker. Over time a screen in the valve can become clogged with sediment and restrict water flow. Another possible cause is a broken solenoid that opens the valve and controls water flow.

CONSIDER THIS

First, check that there isn't a visible kink or blockage in the water supply line. Inspect the line, which will probably run from under the sink or from the basement to the refrigerator—it may simply be pinched behind the fridge—or so we can hope! Most of the line will likely be hidden, but it's always best to rule out the obvious first.

PREP WORK

- Pull the refrigerator away from the wall and unplug it.
- Locate the shut-off valve supplying water to the maker. There will likely be a saddle valve on a cold water pipe; turn off the water (a).
- Locate the access panel behind the fridge—remove it, revealing the water valve assembly.

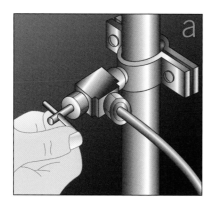

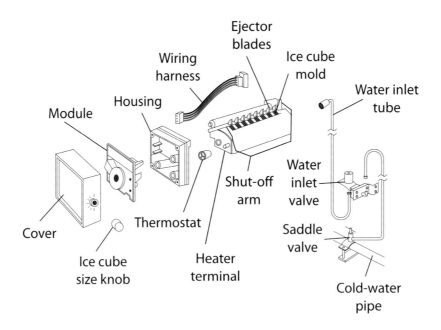

Ejector blades

Wiring harness

Ice cube mold

Water inlet tube

Module

Housing

Cover

Ice cube size knob

Thermostat

Heater terminal

Shut-off arm

Water inlet valve

Saddle valve

Cold-water pipe

THE PROJECT

1 Disconnect the fill tube from the inlet valve—use a wrench to unscrew the nut and gently pull it aside. Be ready with a small bucket to catch water remaining in the line that'll spill.

2 Unplug the solenoid wires from the valve.

3 Unscrew the bracket securing the water valve to the refrigerator wall and remove the unit.

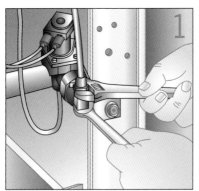

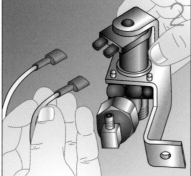

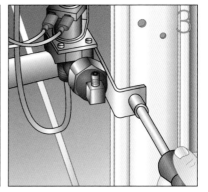

4 With a multimeter, test to see if the solenoid is still functioning. Set the meter to test resistance (ohm)—RX-100. Touch the tester probes to each terminal. It should read between 200 and 500 ohm. If it reads "infinite" or the needle doesn't move, that means the solenoid is broken and will need to be replaced. At this point, it makes sense to change the entire valve. Contact the manufacturer or an appliance center for the proper replacement.

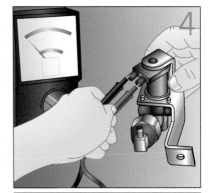

5 Now you need to check and clean the valve filter screen for sediment. With a wrench, unscrew the large fitting where the water enters the valve.

6 Gently pry out the screen. Brush it with an old toothbrush and rinse it with water.

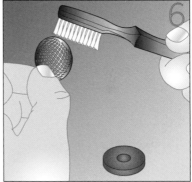

7 Pop the screen back in place and screw the assembly back together.

8 Turn the water back on and check for leaks.

Cabinets

Don't throw out the baby with the bathwater. Your cabinets may very well be worth saving. Refinishing your cabinets is a big job, but costs a fraction of what it would to replace them. Check out this project to see if refinishing makes more sense than tearing out and replacing.

Refinish Wood Cabinets

WHAT YOU'LL NEED

Screwdrivers

Drill/driver

Newspaper and/or dropcloth

Masking tape

Protective hand and eye gear

Chemical stripper

Brushes (synthetic and/or natural, as recommended)

Putty knife (with tips filed down to avoid gouging wood)

Various paint scrapers

Mineral spirits

Steel wool

Fine sandpaper

Clean rags

Rollers

Paint pans

Primer and paint*

Stain*

Stain sealer*

Protective finish*

* If applicable

Although it's labor intensive, refinishing cabinets is an extremely effective way to renew the look of your kitchen, and at a fraction of the cost of replacing them. Of course, first you have to ask yourself whether it's worth it—in other words, is the quality of your cabinets worth investing all the time that will go into refinishing them? Will the end result significantly improve the way they look? Obviously, if you have particle-board cabinets that are old and damaged, refinishing them won't make much of a difference; they likely won't even hold up to the stripping process. (If that's the case, until you're ready to install new cabinets, give them a quick cleaning, sanding, and painting, and call it a day.)

If you have wood cabinets that are deeply blemished—scratched, chipping, and so on—but otherwise in stable condition, refinishing is a great option. The refinishing process removes the old finish—stripping the existing paint, varnish, and/or shellac—and brings the wood down to its natural state. At that point, you can apply an entirely new finish. This blank slate is where you have freedom to give your old cabinets just about any new look you desire.

CONSIDER THIS

Refinishing cabinets is hard work and time-consuming. It must take place over the course of several days, even if you're refinishing just one cabinet. Of course, the more cabinets you have, the longer it'll take. Because of various stripping processes, it's a messy job as well. Be prepared for your kitchen to be pretty much off-limits to food preparation and eating for the duration of the project.

You'll need a clean workspace to refinish the doors and drawers because you'll remove them from the cabinets for this project. It is crucial that this area be as dust free as possible to prevent particles from sticking to the wet surfaces.

Using a chemical stripper is typically the fastest and easiest way to remove a finish. It's important to let the chemical reaction of the stripping agent work after it's applied to the surface. Don't try to muscle off the old finish. Some sanding will likely be necessary at the end of the stripping process.

Many different types of chemical strippers are available. Use one that is environmentally safer, cleans up with water, doesn't raise the wood grain, and clings well to vertical surfaces (like Allov-It by Rock-Miracle).

Most chemical paint strippers give off noxious vapors. Be sure to work in a well-ventilated area, wear safety gear, and follow all manufacturer's instructions and safety precautions.

If your cabinets have a lot of detail, invest in paint scrapers fitted with different-shape blades to get in all the various grooves.

PREP WORK

- Remove articles from the countertops and inside the cabinets.

- Spread newspaper or a dropcloth beneath the cabinets, including the floors.

- Remove all the hardware—storing all hinges, screws, and pulls/knobs in a safe place.

- Remove the drawers and move them, along with the doors, to a protected work surface. Label and number each drawer and door with masking tape—this will help to keep track of where the drawers and door will be go. Trust me, it can get very confusing! Keep the label by its side while working each surface.

- If you want to replace the old knobs and pulls, now is the time to work on new hole placement if necessary (see "Add or Replace Knobs and Pulls" on page 40).

THE PROJECT

REMOVE THE OLD FINISH

1. Acquaint yourself with chemical stripper. Read all instructions and safety precautions.

2. Apply the product to the surface in a thick layer—typically it's brushed on. Let it set for the recommended time. (Don't spread the product over too large a surface at once—you want it to remain wet while you're scraping.)

3. After it has set the recommended time, at an angle push the scraper through the old finish—it should slough off like gooey pudding—until the putty knife reaches the wood. Be careful not to gouge the wood while you're scraping. Discard the old finish as it accumulates on the knife. If there is a thick finish, you'll likely need to repeat these steps until reaching the raw wood. Scrape in the direction of the wood grain.

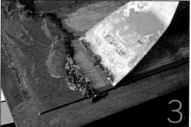

4 Use steel wool to rub out stubborn spots—apply the stripper to the spot first. If stains remain, try wood bleach, following the manufacturer's instructions.

5 After all the finish has been removed, wipe away any residue with mineral spirits. (Some strippers can be cleaned up with water, but water could also soak into the wood and cause it to swell and raise the grain, so opt for mineral spirits instead.)

6 Allow all the surfaces to dry.

CHOOSE AND APPLY THE NEW FINISH

At this point, there are many different finishes that may be applied to your cabinets. Application process, look, and durability will vary according to the finish you choose. Explore the following finish options. Whichever finish you choose, be sure all your surfaces are clean and dry before applying the new finish.

Paint

Painting your cabinets offers a wide range of color choices and, depending on the paint finish, can provide excellent durability, especially scrub-ability. Painted cabinets are a great choice when the cabinet wood itself is not attractive. Be sure to choose a primer and painter with formulas specific to this type of application—such as BEHR Premium Plus Interior Enamel Undercoater Primer & Sealer No. 75 followed by BEHR Premium Plus Interior Kitchen & Bath Sateen Lustre Enamel. Whichever primer and paint you choose, be sure to follow the manufacturer's instructions and safety precautions.

1 Proper priming is crucial for excellent results. Apply primer to all of the surfaces and allow it to dry. First, cut all the edges, grooves, and corners with a brush. Then roll the primer over the large surfaces. Always check for drip marks on the vertical surfaces and smooth them out with a brush. Be sure to smooth out any ridges or roller marks with a light brush stroke.

2 Choose a paint that is impervious to stain and has high resistance to scrubbing. Typically, the shinier the finish, the more durable. Follow the same painting techniques as directed for the primer. Allow the first coat to dry. For the doors, be sure that one side is totally dry before flipping it to paint the other.

3 If necessary, apply a second coat. The manufacturer may recommend lightly sanding the first coat before applying the second. Be sure the surface is dust free before repainting.

Stain

If you want to keep the wood look of your cabinets, you'll likely want to stain them to unify the color of the wood. Remember that staining simply applies color and does not provide a protective finish. Stain, unlike paint, actually soaks into the wood and alters its color. Additionally, some stains enhance the wood-grain characteristics, while others conceal them—from transparent to semi-transparent, semi-opaque to opaque. Although staining wood a lighter color is complicated (it involves a lengthy process of wood bleaching), going from light to dark is simple. Depth of color can be intensified by applying additional coats of stain. Because stain pertains to color, a protective finish must be applied after the staining process is complete. Some stains, however, offer a finish in their formula creating a one-step process, but these products may not offer a superior-looking finish.

1 Before applying stain, you must condition the wood with a sealer. This product will help the stain soak in uniformly. Apply an ample coat of sealer according to the manufacturer's instructions. Wipe away any excess with a clean rag. Allow the product to dry before staining.

2 Follow the manufacturer's instructions for applying the stain. Generally, the stain is brushed on or rubbed into the wood with a rag. The excess is wiped off with a clean rag. To darken and intensify the stain, these steps may be repeated.

ADD A PROTECTIVE FINISH

Once the stain has dried, a protective finish must be applied. Stained wood can be finished in a variety of ways with varying degrees of difficulty and durability. *Penetrating oil,* like Tung or Danish oil, is easy to apply and offers a very subtle and natural finish, but it doesn't offer much wood protection for the wear and tear of a kitchen. *Lacquer* finish is rich and durable, but it's tricky to execute because of its rapid drying time and finicky nature. *Oil-based polyurethane and water-based polyurethanes* are excellent finishes for kitchen cabinets because of their ease of application and durability—oil based is the most durable.

1 Follow the manufacturer's instructions for applying either water-based or oil-based polyurethane. Generally, you apply a thin coat with a brush—natural bristle for oil-based, synthetic for water-based. Be sure to stir the polyurethane before and during application to avoid settling. Do not shake the can!

2 Allow the coat to dry. Lightly sand the surfaces with fine sandpaper. Wipe away any dust with a clean rag.

3 Apply the second coat. Repeat these steps if a third coat is recommended.

4 Allow at least 24 hours to pass after applying the final coat before reinstalling the doors and drawers.

FINISH THE JOB

After all the cabinet surfaces are thoroughly dry, install the hardware.

- To rehang the doors, first hang the hinges on the door and then on the door frame.
- Use the screw in the small adjustment slot of the door hardware to raise or lower the doors for perfect alignment.
- If the drawers are sticky when opening and closing, spray some Teflon lubricant on the rails.

Walls and Floors

New track lighting here, a newly refinished floor there . . . updates like these can make your kitchen feel like a whole new space.

Install a Task Light Fixture

WHAT YOU'LL NEED

New flexible-track low-volt light kit

Flathead and Phillips screwdrivers

Lineman pliers

Hammer

Utility knife

Pencil

Paper

Tape measure

Non-contact voltage tester (pen type)

Typically, a kitchen will have one overhead light. This type of fixture may be fine for general illumination, but in kitchens we often require light directed to where we really need it—like over the sink or cutting board.

Today, track lighting has become so versatile and adaptable; from one fixture you can customize lighting to meet both general and task. What's also great about building your own track lighting system? It can be wired through your existing electrical box—no additional electric lines need to be added. As for the track, it's simply mounted to the ceiling at strategic points. Because electric current runs through the track, fixtures or pendants are "quick-connected" right to it. I especially like flexible-line track kits because you can really custom-shape the track to whatever form fits your room and illumination needs. Finally, this type of track lighting immediately updates the look of your kitchen because of its sleek styling.

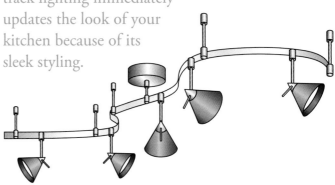

CONSIDER THIS

Flexible-line track kits come in *line-volt* and *low-volt*. The power source comes from the track itself, but line-volt runs standard 120V through the track, while the low-volt uses a transformer for low-voltage fixtures.

Flex kits are adjustable in length, and fixtures may be added—the manufacturer will indicate maximum wattage. These features allow you to easily make changes to the unit even after it's been installed—perfect if you ever think you need more light over a particular section of counter, for example.

The first rule of any electric project is to shut off the power from the breaker or fuse box. Putting the light switch to the off position does not offer enough protection. Switches are accidentally flipped on, and other live wires may be in the fixture's electric box—that's why shutting power from the service panel is crucial for your safety.

Once the power is off at the panel, be sure that no one will turn the power on as you're working.

If you're unsure which breaker or fuse controls your bathroom fixture, here's what to do: Working with a partner, put the light on. Begin flipping breakers on and off as someone is monitoring the light. When the light shuts off, have them yell to you, and mark the breaker.

PREP WORK: REMOVE THE OLD FIXTURE

- First, shut the power off to the light from the service panel.

- Removing the old fixture will vary depending on what type of light you have. Generally, you'll first need to remove the globe or light cover and then the bulbs.

- Once the globe and bulb(s) are removed, there may be nuts that secure the fixture base to the wall. Unscrew them and pull the fixture away from the wall. If it has been caulked or painted, it may help to run a utility knife around the seam where the fixture meets the wall (being careful not to damage the wall).

- Pulling out the fixture should reveal wires, an electrical box, and potentially a round mounting plate or strap. Mentally note how the wires are connected (usually black to black, white to white, ground to ground), because you'll need to repeat the same wiring.

- With a non-contact voltage tester, test that the power is off. Hold the tester up to the wires—no light or ringing indicates no power.

- Unscrew the wire nuts and disconnect the fixture. Set the fixture aside. It's good practice to reconnect the wire nuts to the now-single wires (a).

- If there's a mounting plate that is similar to the new one, you may leave the old one in. If not, remove it.

- A bare copper ground wire may be screwed to the inside of the electrical box—disconnect it.

- You should now have a black, white, and ground wire (copper or green) coming out of your electric box.

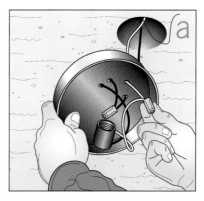

THE PROJECT

Installing a new fixture will vary depending on its brand. The following are general instructions on how to install a flexible low-volt track-light kit. Always follow the manufacturer's instructions and safety precautions. **Note:** Low-volt track lights have a transformer that will be wired with the unit.

1 Familiarize yourself with the parts of your new fixture.

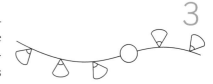

2 With the power off at the service panel, recheck the exposed wires with an electric tester to verify that the power is off.

3 Make a sketch of how you would like to shape the fixture. Take a measurement of approximately how much length you'll need. Keep in mind where the electrical box is located in the ceiling.

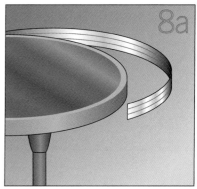

4 Make the electrical connections from the unit (in this case the transformer) to the electrical box—black to black, white to white, ground to ground, or ground to electrical box. Be sure that your wires are properly connected and tightened with wire nuts. (If you tug on the wire nuts, they shouldn't be able to pull off—either screw them on tighter or use smaller wire nuts.)

5 Carefully fold the wires up into the electrical box.

6 Secure the unit's mounting plate to the electrical box—line up the holes of the plate to the box and screw it in place.

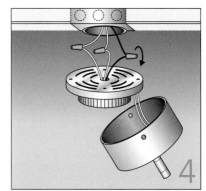

7 Secure the transformer housing to the mounting plate.

8 Address the rail:

- The rail will bend by hand. Use a curved object, like a round table or garbage pail, to make the desired curves along the rail (a).

- The rail may be cut to length using a hacksaw and finished with an end cap.

- With a partner, hold the rail up to the ceiling in line with the transformer and mark the corresponding support bracket located on the rail to the ceiling (b). **Note:** The transformer will act as a support as well.

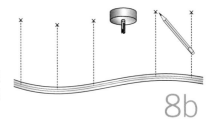

- Tap anchors into the ceiling at each mark (c).
- Screw the mounting brackets (also called *standoffs*) to each anchor (d).
- Twist each mounting bracket so its direction fits in line with the rail.
- With a partner, raise the rail to the brackets, lining them up (e).
- Attach the provided mounting caps to each bracket that secure the brackets to the rail. **Note:** Each mounting bracket will have a cap that should not be interchanged with the mounting cap designated for the transformer. There will be a plastic insulator in the bracket that meets the rail—be sure it's in place (f).

9 Hang the fixtures:

- Assemble the fixture as instructed, attaching the globe and so on.
- Raise the fixture to the rail at the desired position and connect it to the rail. Again, be sure that the plastic insulator in the fixture bracket is in place, or you risk burning out the transformer. Check that the connection is tight.
- Repeat the prior step with each fixture.

10 Turn on the light and leave it on for several minutes. Turn it off, and check to see if any of the connections feel hot. If so, tighten them.

11 Pivot each fixture to illuminate the desired area.

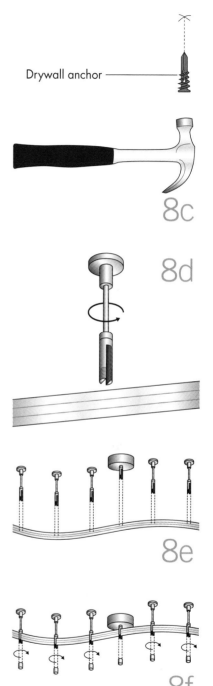

Drywall anchor

8c

8d

8e

8f

Refinish Wood Floors

WHAT YOU'LL NEED

Drum sander

Edge sanders

Orbital sander

Hammer*

Nail set*

Putty knife*

Scraper

Tape measure

Plastic dropcloths

Masking tape

Painter's tape

Stainable wood filler*

Spiral shank nails*

Extension cords

Dust mask or respirator

Earplugs

Safety goggles

Sandpaper sheets fitted for specific sanders—coarse, medium, and fine grit

Sandpaper blocks—coarse, medium, and fine grit

Latex or rubber gloves

Vacuum cleaner

Wood stain of choice

4-inch brush (suitable for stain choice)

Cotton rags

Tack cloths (suitable for water or oil-based finish)

Polyurethane (oil-based) **or urethane** (water-based) **finish**

Paint tray

Small and large applicator pads or 4-inch paintbrush

Vacuum cleaner

Paint thinner (for polyurethane cleanup)*

* If applicable

Wood floors in a kitchen are wonderful in so many ways—they're easy on the feet, won't cause dropped dishes or glasses to shatter (like tile), and so on. However, when it comes to durability, between heavy traffic and spills, they can really take a beating. If they aren't properly maintained, refinishing them will be the only way to restore their good looks.

A floor will need to be refinished when deep scratches are present, large sections are worn down to the wood, and staining and darkening have occurred. If your floor is dull, with minor scratches and worn spots here and there, resealing your floor may be all that's necessary (see "Reseal a Damaged Wood Floor Section" on page 51).

The refinishing process removes the old finish—sanding away the existing shellac, polyurethane, and so on—and brings the wood down to its natural state. At that point, an entirely new stain and finish is applied.

CONSIDER THIS

There's no other way to say this—refinishing floors is a *big* job. It's extremely labor intensive, hard on the body, and takes several days to complete. Count on your kitchen being out of commission for potentially over a week. The size of your kitchen and number of coats needed will determine how long the process will actually take.

The refinishing process requires a lot of sanding. Be prepared to seal off the area with plastic dropcloths and use proper safety gear.

Floors cannot be refinished repeatedly—they must be ¾-inch thick. If you're unsure if the floor has been sanded before or how thick it is, take a look at the edges and use a tape measure to check—perhaps around a heat register or molding. You don't want to accidentally sand down to the subfloor. If your floor is less than ¾-inch thick, call in the pros.

PREP WORK

- Remove everything possible from the space. If the floor extends into a closet or pantry, remove everything from in there as well.

- Protect the cabinets and fixtures with dropcloths.

- Cover windows, outlets, switches, and vent ducts with painter's tape and plastic (closing the ducts first).

- Seal off the kitchen from the rest of the house with a large plastic dropcloth and masking tape.

- Remove any shoe molding (a). Baseboards may be left alone.

- Give the floor a good inspection. Are there any loose boards? Any nails popping up? Are there any cracks that need filling? If so, make all repairs now. Loose boards may be secured down with spiral-shank flooring nails, countersunk with a nail set, and then filled in with wood filler. Use a scraper and filler to fill in cracks.

- Give the floor a good vacuum.

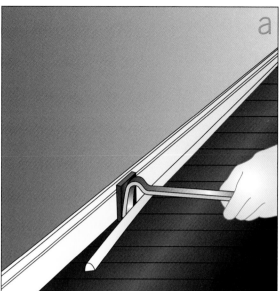

THE PROJECT

You'll need specialized sanding equipment that can be rented from hardware and rental centers, namely a drum sander and an edge sander. I highly recommend practicing with them first on a piece of plywood and getting a feel for their handling with the power off first. This equipment is loud and cumbersome, but with practice, it'll yield results you could never accomplish by hand or with smaller equipment.

The most important thing to remember is *keep the sander moving*. Don't let it sit in one area because it can quickly make a gouge or swirl right through to the subfloor.

STAGE 1: USING THE DRUM SANDER

1 Familiarize yourself with the equipment and observe all safety warnings.

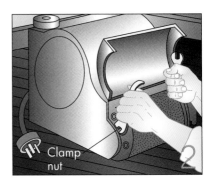

Clamp nut

2 Load the sander with appropriate-grit sandpaper—typically 20- to 60-grit to start with, and work to 120-grit (the higher the grit, the finer the sandpaper). Typical sandpaper loading will vary depending on the type of equipment you've rented. The following are basic instructions for loading the sandpaper:

- With the sander *unplugged,* turn it over and locate the loading slot in the drum.

- Slip an end of the sandpaper sheet into the slot. Spin the drum a full revolution and slip the other end of the sheet into the slot.

- Tighten down the nuts or clamps located on either end of the drum.

- The paper should be snug, but not overly taught or compressing the drum rubber. **Note:** As the paper becomes worn after several passes, the sanding will diminish. When you see this happening, reload the sander with a fresh sheet.

3 Put on your safety gear (earplugs, goggles, and dust mask).

4 Your starting position with the sander should be at the right side of the room. (You'll be working from right to left.) The sander should be placed in the same direction as the wood grain and approximately two-thirds of the room should be in front of you. With the sander tilted back, turn it on and let it spin to full speed. Gently lower it to the floor as you slowly start walking forward. Keep a steady, even pace. As you approach the wall, slowly tilt the sander back. Always keep the sander moving when it's in contact with the floor.

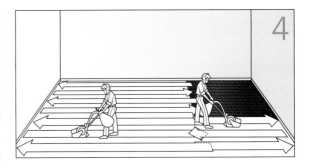

5 Walking backward, resand the same path you made following the above steps.

6 When you're back to your original starting point, gently tilt the machine back and move it to the left about 3 to 4 inches. Lower the machine, which will slightly overlap the path you just made, and repeat the forward and backward pass.

7 Continue these steps until you reach the left side of the room.

8 Start the process over for the remaining one-third section of floor, moving the sander to the right side of the room and repeating the forward-and-backward passes. Be sure to overlap onto the two-thirds section (you've already completed) by a couple of feet in order to properly blend the two areas.

9 Once you've completed the entire floor, vacuum.

Note: The initial sanding passes (with the coarse paper) should clean and sand the floor to the wood. If it doesn't after a forward and backward pass, switch to a coarser paper. (The finer-grit papers that you'll use later smooth the scratches made by the first pass.)

There will be a border of unsanded floor that the drum sander couldn't reach. You'll sand these sections with an edge sander.

STAGE 2: USING THE EDGE SANDER

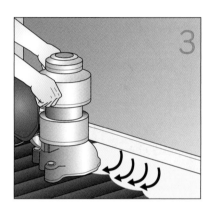

1 Load the edge sander with a slightly less-coarse paper than what you started with on the drum sander.

2 Along the long direction of flooring, run the sander in long, steady passes—back and forth—following the same technique as the drum sander. Be sure to overlap onto the drum-sanded area.

3 Where the plank ends butt to the wall, use a semicircular motion when sanding with the end stroke going along the wood grain and overlapping the drum-sanded area.

4 Vacuum the entire area.

STAGE 3: ORBITAL SANDING, HAND-SCRAPING, AND SANDING

There will be corners and other areas (such as around a radiator) where the edge sander will not reach.

1 For hard-to-reach areas, use a small orbital or detail sander. Use your hand to feel that the same level of sanding is achieved between these areas and what has already been sanded smooth.

2 For harder-to-reach areas, hand-scraping and sanding will be necessary. When using a scraper, be careful not to gouge the wood. Always work in the direction of the grain.

3 Use sanding blocks for final finish removal, again starting with coarse, but later working to fine.

STAGE 4: FINISHING THE SANDING PROCESS

1 After the entire floor surface has been sanded with the coarse paper, repeat Stages 1–3, but this time move to a medium-grit sandpaper.

2 Check areas that have been repaired with wood putty and refill them if necessary.

3 Once the entire floor has been sanded with medium-grit sandpaper, move to the fine grit and repeat the entire process.

4 Remove the protective covers around the room and vacuum the entire area and floor vigorously. Wipe down the floor with a tack cloth (choose a tack cloth that is suitable for the type of finish you choose).

5 Don't walk on the floor with shoes—the raw wood is very vulnerable to marring.

STAINING

Staining your floor is optional; however, it's a popular choice because of the vast variety of colors. Whichever color or type of stain you choose, follow the manufacturer's directions and safety precautions. Here are some additional tips:

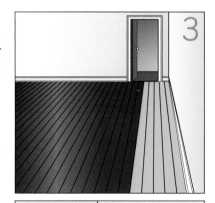

1 Work in a well-ventilated area.

2 Test the stain color in a hidden area before applying to the entire floor.

3 Work from one end of the room to the other end of the room.

4 It's easiest to work with a partner—one person applies the stain while the other wipes it away.

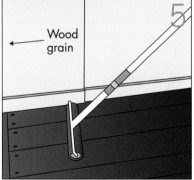

5 Work in the stain with the direction of the wood grain. The longer the stain sits, the deeper the color will become.

6 Do not let the stain pool in one area when it's being applied.

7 Repeat coats if recommended by the manufacturer.

8 Let the stain dry overnight and do not walk on it.

APPLY THE PROTECTIVE FINISH

Several types of finishes may be applied to protect your floor. Today, water-based urethane surface finishes are very durable, easy to work with, and better for the environment. They come in matte, satin, semigloss, and high-gloss finishes. Polyurethane is the oil-based version of this product. Whichever type of finish you choose, follow the manufacturer's directions and safety precautions. Here are some additional tips:

1 Work in a ventilated area.

2 Stir the can—do not shake it—and do so regularly during the application to avoid settling.

3 Brush the finish along the perimeter of the floor with a wide bristle brush.

4 Starting from the far end of the room and working toward the door, apply the finish to the floor with a brush or applicator pad, working in 5-foot-long sections. (Vacuum the applicator pad before using it to remove any loose fibers.)

5 Be careful to avoid drips and thick overlaps of the finish—smooth these out immediately.

6 Allow to dry. Then, by hand, lightly sand with fine-grit sandpaper. Vacuum thoroughly.

7 Repeat Steps 2–6 until the desired number of coats has been applied.

Part 3

Intensive Treatment

Sinks

The sink/faucet combo is a major work and focal point of your kitchen. Replacing them is a wise investment that will update the look and increase the functionality of your kitchen. To step it up a notch further, adding a water purifier is a smart way to bring quality water to your home. Check out these projects to make your sink station an absolute oasis.

Install a New Faucet

WHAT YOU'LL NEED

New faucet

Basin wrench

Tongue-and-groove pliers

Adjustable wrench

Installation tool*

Flashlight

Pillow or large kneeling pad

Scour pad

Rags

Penetrating oil

New stainless-steel braided water supply lines*

Teflon tape*

Plumber's putty*

* If applicable

Sometimes, the hardest part of installing a new faucet is removing the old one. Mineral deposits build up around old fittings, making it tough to disconnect the faucet from the sink deck. Be prepared to go to battle with your old faucet if it's been there a while, especially if you have hard water in your area.

CONSIDER THIS

The most important detail to know when choosing a new faucet is what kind of faucet your sink/countertop can accommodate. Are you mounting into your sink or your countertop? How many holes does it have? It helps to take a photo of your old faucet to help with choosing a new one, or take the old faucet with you to the store.

Spout length and height are crucial elements because these affect how the water falls into the sink. The depth of your basin also affects how the water falls. Keep in mind that the higher the spout and the shallower the basin, the more the water will splash outside of the sink.

Working under a sink can disorient your sense of *lefty loosey, righty tighty*. Make sure you're unscrewing the old parts in the right direction.

Before starting this project, check to see that the shut-off valve is working properly (see "Replace a Shut-Off Valve" on page 108).

With any faucet, always read the manufacturer's installation instructions and safety precautions.

PREP WORK: REMOVE THE OLD FAUCET

- Clear away everything from under your sink for a clutter-free workspace.

- Set a flashlight under the faucet and place a pillow or kneeling pad under you to work comfortably.

- Shut off the water from the shut-off valves.

- Turn the water on at the faucet to relieve pressure.

- Unscrew the water supply line from the faucet and shut-off valves.

- Spray the mounting nuts with penetrating oil and let it soak in.

- With a basin wrench, unscrew the mounting/locking nuts (a).

- Pull out the old faucet (b).

THE PROJECT

1 Read your faucet's instructions and safety precautions. Acquaint yourself with your faucet parts.

2 Using a scour pad, clean away residue on your sink or vanity that may remain from the old faucet. **Note:** If you're installing a new sink as well, it's easier to install the faucet (water supply lines and all) to the sink before mounting the sink in the countertop. If this is the case, work on a padded surface to protect the sink as you install the faucet to it.

3 Assemble your faucet as directed in its instructions.

4 A faucet will use either a gasket or plumber's putty to create a seal between it and the deck. Insert the gasket as directed or apply plumber's putty under the faucet. (Roll room-temperature putty in your hands to make a string of it, and press it around the perimeter of the faucet—enough so that when you press the faucet in place excess squeezes out.)

5 Guide the faucet into the deck hole(s). Orient the faucet so the handles/spout face the right direction. If using putty, press firmly.

6 Thread and tighten the mounting/locking nut(s) or plate under the sink with a basin wrench or pliers. (Some faucets provide their own specialized installation tool for this.) Remove excess putty that may squeeze out.

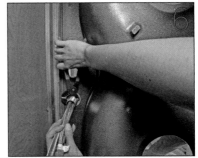

7 Gently spread the faucet inlets so they're approximately 2 inches apart.

8 If recommended, wrap Teflon tape around the inlet threads. Looking from underneath, wrap the tape clockwise (the same direction as you'll be tightening the supply lines).

9 If your faucet has a sprayer, feed the sprayer hose down the faucet.

10 Now you can connect all the supply lines. Screw the hot and cold supply lines to the inlets (a). Then screw them to the shut-offs with an adjustable wrench or pliers (b). Don't let the lines spin as you're tightening them, and make sure you connect hot to hot and cold to cold. Connect the sprayer hose—some faucets come with a snap-together type connector where no screwing is necessary.

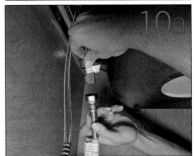

11 The sprayer will have a counterweight that attaches to the hose that allows it to move smoothly and retract back as you use it. See the manufacturer's instructions on how this weight is installed.

12 Turn the water on at the shut-off valves and check for leaks at each connection.

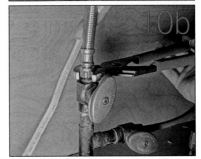

13 Let the water run from the faucet to clear out any debris—again, check for leaks.

14 Screw on the aerator and/or sprayer. Turn on the faucet and verify that they're flowing/spraying properly.

Replace a Shut-Off Valve

WHAT YOU'LL NEED

Replacement shut-off valve

Two pairs of tongue-and-groove pliers

Mini pipe cutter

Additional pipe and coupling*

Plumber's torch*

Handheld propane gas canister

Sandpaper*

Heat-resistant shield and gloves*

* If applicable

Often, when working on a sink project, you'll go to shut off the water from the valve to get started and hit a major roadblock—a valve leaks, ugh! The only thing to do is replace it, since a leaky shut-off valve is the first sign of it failing completely—not to mention that you can't get started on that sink project.

If you live in an older home, I highly recommend inspecting all your shut-off valves (to your toilets, washing machine, and so on). Go ahead and replace your shut-off valves if

- Mineral deposits are built up along the valve.
- They drip when you turn them off.
- You can't turn the handle at all because it's seized in the open position.

It's always better to install new shut-off valves when you're not *forced* to. Additionally, if only one of the valves is leaking (either the hot or cold), go ahead and replace both of them. It's only a matter of time before the second one will begin to leak.

CONSIDER THIS

Replacing a shut-off valve requires shutting down water to the house from the water main. Once you remove that valve, it must be replaced or capped in order for water to be restored to the house.

Examine your existing shut-off. Is it copper pipe or galvanized? Is it a straight-stop or angle-stop? Is it soldered on or is it a compression fitting? You must know all these details in order to purchase the proper replacement.

Sometimes it's best to take the old shut-off valve with you to the store, but know that the water main will have to remain off until you cap or replace the valve.

This project shows installing a ¼-turn angle-stop compression-type shut-off valve onto a copper stub-out.

PREP WORK

- Shut off the water from the water main.

- Drain the system by opening a faucet at a fixture above the shut-off valve and at the lowest point of the house.

TO REMOVE A SOLDERED SHUT-OFF

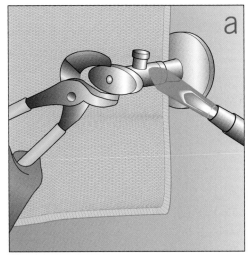

- If you have extra pipe to spare on the stub-out, you can simply cut off the old valve with a pipe cutter. To use the cutter, open its jaws so the pipe fits in its curve. Tighten the cutter onto the pipe as close to the old valve as possible. When it's snug, spin the cutter around the pipe. As the cutter wheel scores the pipe, gradually tighten it so it cuts deeper, until it slices all the way through.

- If you don't have any extra pipe, you'll need to pull off the existing valve from the pipe. With a torch, heat the joint with the valve in the open position. When the solder begins to melt, wiggle off the old valve with pliers (a). Be sure to wear gloves and use a heat-resistant shield to protect the wall. Clean off any excess solder with sandpaper and wipe the pipe clean.

TO REMOVE A COMPRESSION SHUT-OFF

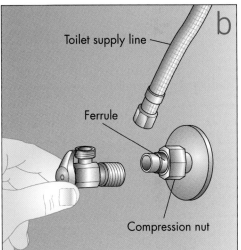

Toilet supply line

Ferrule

Compression nut

- Using two tongue-and-groove pliers, hold back on the stub-out or valve with one pair of pliers and unscrew the compression nut with the other pair of pliers. Unscrewing the valve will require a lot of elbow grease; however, be careful not to wrench so hard that you loosen a fitting behind the wall. When it's unscrewed, you'll find a brass ring (known as a *ferrule*) embedded onto the pipe (b). Leave this there along with the nut to use with the new compression valve. Skip to Step 2.

THE PROJECT

1 Slide the nut, and then the brass ring (ferrule), onto the bare stub-out.

2 Slide the valve onto the pipe until it stops. Rotate the valve on the pipe so that the outlet faces the right direction to accommodate the faucet.

3 Slide the nut back down toward the threads of the valve, wedging the ferrule between it and the valve. **Note:** It is not recommended to use Teflon tape or thread adhesive with compression fittings.

4 With two pairs of tongue-and-groove pliers, hold the valve in place and firmly tighten the nut down.

5 Make sure the valve is in the off position. Turn on the water at the main and check for leaks. **Note:** If using the existing ferrule, it may no longer be able to create a seal. You'll know as soon as the water is turned on. If this is the case, you'll need to cut off that end of pipe, because it will be next to impossible to remove the old ferrule. If there is not enough pipe left on the stub-out, you'll need to sweat on a short length of pipe with a coupling (see the sidebar "How to Sweat Pipe" on the next page).

6 Reconnect the faucet supply line. Turn on the new valve and check for leaks.

How to Sweat Pipe

I know that the name may conjure an image of pipe "sweating" from condensation, but *sweat pipe* is actually a plumbing term used to describe joining copper pipes and fittings together with solder and a torch. As the solder melts around the pipe, it drips as if it were sweating—hence, the name.

When a pipe needs to be lengthened or a fitting (such as an elbow) is needed to configure the direction of a water line, copper fittings are soldered at each joint, which creates a watertight seal.

The process is simple, but it does take some practice. Also, because flame is used, you must take safety precautions. Keep in mind that if you're soldering next to any type of adjoining surface (such as a stud or wall), you need to use a heat-resistant shield to protect it. Be careful not to touch the pipe with your bare hands while it's still hot—use heat-resistant gloves.

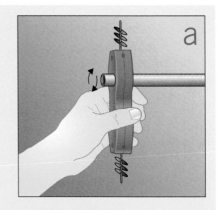

- If you have cut pipe, ream the cut end—insert the short blade into the pipe and firmly give it a few solid turns to remove any burs (a).
- While wearing gloves, clean the ends of the pipe and fitting that will be mated to one another with a specialized wire brush and sandpaper.
- Brush plumbing flux around the abraded surfaces (b).
- Join the pipe and fitting.
- Pull out several inches of solder from its spool.
- Heat the joint with the torch—moving the flame around it (c).
- Just when the flux begins to smoke, move the flame away and press the tip of the solder onto the joint—it will instantly melt and wick into the joint. Touch the solder to the opposing side of the pipe so solder finds its way all the way around the pipe.
- While the joint is still hot, brush some flux over the joint, and then give it a quick wipe with a damp rag.

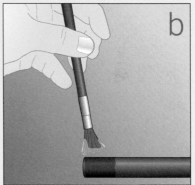

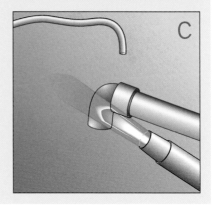

Install an Under-sink Water Filtration System

WHAT YOU'LL NEED

Under-sink dual-carbon-cartridge water filtration kit

Graduated hole saws

Drill/driver

Tongue-and-groove pliers

Hammer

Utility knife

Basin wrench

Masking tape

Marker

Flashlight

Pillow or kneeling pad

Vacuum

Teflon tape

Considering the *billions* of dollars we spend each year on bottled water, installing a water filtration system will not only take a dent out of your wallet, but help the environment by minimizing the tons of plastic water bottles we end up tossing away.

Many different types of purifying systems exist, varying in method, performance, and price, but an under-sink dual-carbon-cartridge water filtration system is easy to install and will reduce odor and improve taste. Furthermore, carbon, known for its ability to absorb impurities, will filter the most common contaminants and chemicals found in some municipal tap water.

CONSIDER THIS

You may want to have your water tested by certified laboratory in your area for a detailed analysis of contaminants that may be in your tap water.

The filtration system described in this project requires that an additional hole be present on your sink deck or countertop to accommodate a new filter faucet.

Carbon filters require periodic replacement—typically once every 6 months.

Water filtration systems vary in how they're installed. This project shows the installation of an under-sink drinking water filtration kit that taps into the cold water supply with a manufacturer-supplied T-fitting. It also uses an *open relief faucet* that keeps pressure out of the filter until water is demanded. Always follow the manufacturer's instructions and safety precautions.

PREP WORK

- Familiarize yourself with the contents of your filtration system.

- Clear away everything from under your sink for a clutter-free workspace.

- Set a flashlight under the faucet and place a pillow or kneeling pad under you to work comfortably.

- Shut off the cold water supply to the faucet at the shut-off valve (a).

- Turn the water on at the faucet to relieve pressure and empty the line.

- Unscrew the cold water supply line from the shut-off valve.

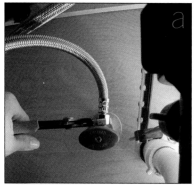

THE PROJECT

1 Determine where the filter faucet will be positioned. Some sinks provide additional holes for a sprayer, soap dispenser, or water filter faucet. If your sink does not have one, you can drill a hole through the sink according to the manufacturer's hole size—that is, provided your sink is stainless steel. (Porcelain-coated cast iron and porcelain sinks are very challenging to drill through.) Another option would be to drill the hole through your countertop, right next to the sink. Wherever the location, be sure that the spout extends slightly past the sink edge.

To drill through a stainless-steel sink:

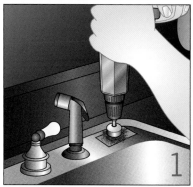

- Choose a series of hole saws where the largest bit accommodates the faucet (as indicated by the manufacturer).

- Place masking tape at the center of the hole site (to help prevent the bit from "walking").

- Start with a ½-inch hole saw bit and graduate each cut a ⅛ inch until you reach the faucet hole size. Be sure to wear safety glasses.

- Vacuum away all debris from drilling.

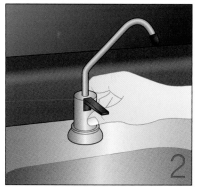

2 Fit any supplied washers and escutcheons onto the bottom of the filter faucet and guide the unit through the hole.

3 From under the cabinet, secure the faucet to the sink with the supplied mounting bracket, washer, and nut. Use a basin wrench to screw it snug.

4 Find a location under the cabinet to mount the filter bracket. Position it in a spot where the tubing will not kink or have to bend with any kind of pressure running from the filter faucet to the filter. A good position is somewhere between the cold water supply and the filter faucet. Remember to allow for any specified clearance that is required when replacing the cartridges. Use the supplied screws and anchors to mount the bracket into the cabinet or wall.

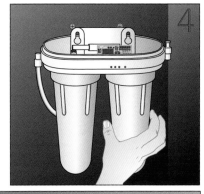

5 Wrap Teflon tape around the threads of the shut-off valve, turning the tape in the same direction you'll be screwing on the T-fitting. Give the tape a few spins and be sure not to obstruct the opening.

6 Hand-screw the T onto the shut-off valve, and snug it with tongue-and-groove pliers or a wrench.

7 Wrap Teflon around the top opening of the T and rescrew the water supply line to your main faucet.

8 Cut a length of tubing supplied by the manufacturer that will run from the T to the faucet valve (where the handle is, pictured as red tube).

9 This tubing connects to the T with a compression fitting. Slide the nut and brass ring (ferrule) onto the tubing, and screw the nut to the T. Snug it tight.

10 To attach the tubing to the faucet, push the tubing into the indicated inlet port for the faucet valve. These tubes simply push to connect.

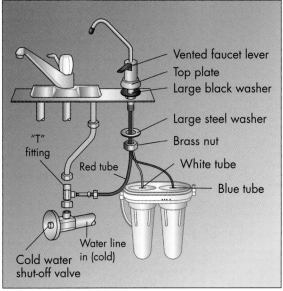

Vented faucet lever
Top plate
Large black washer

Large steel washer

Brass nut

"T" fitting

Red tube

White tube

Blue tube

Water line in (cold)

Cold water shut-off valve

11 Cut two more lengths of tubing: one that will run from the valve to the intake filter (pictured as white tube), and another that will run from the outlet filter and up the gooseneck of the faucet spout (pictured as blue tube). **Note:** Units that do not have an open relief faucet will simply have two tubes: one for the inlet port and one for the outlet.

12 Turn the cold water on at the shut-off valve and check for leaks at all connections.

13 Lift the valve lever and allow the water to run until all bubbles and cloudiness disappear.

Install a New Drop-in Sink

WHAT YOU'LL NEED

New drop-in sink (self-rimming)

Basin wrench

Screwdrivers

Drill/driver

Tongue-and-groove pliers

Adjustable wrench

Utility knife

Folding handsaw fitted with a 6-inch reciprocating metal blade

Close-quarter hacksaw or reciprocating saw with 6-inch bimetal blade*

Hacksaw

⅜-inch drill bit for jigsaw starter hole

Jigsaw (with blade according to your countertop material)

Safety glasses

Flashlight

Pillow or large kneeling pad

Small bucket

Scour pad

Rags

Penetrating oil

Cardboard

Level

Pencil and marker

Tape measure

Drain adapter*

Faucet and new stainless-steel braided water supply lines*

Drain setup, including strainer basket, tailpiece, P-trap, and adapter and rubber coupler*—PVC or ABS with slip-joint fittings

Teflon tape

Plumber's putty*

Pipe joint compound

Silicone or caulking adhesive

Caulking gun

* If applicable

Whether your existing sink is chipped and worn or you just want to update the look of your kitchen, the drop-in sinks available today are attractive and plentiful. Because they're self-rimming, installation is quite straightforward.

CONSIDER THIS

When choosing a new drop-in sink, consider the following

- Do you need a sink with faucet holes, or does your faucet mount to your countertop?

- What is the size of the cutout for your existing sink? You must choose a sink that size or larger (unless you're replacing the countertop as well).

- Is it truly "drop-in," meaning it's self-rimming? This nature makes it a simple and compatible replacement to your existing vanity.

- Do you want a sink with more than one bowl?

- Would a built-in drain board suit your needs?

Be sure to know the dimensions of your existing opening—unless you're replacing the countertop, you'll need a sink that is the same size as, or larger than, your existing one.

If your countertop is natural stone or tiled, I recommend finding a sink with the same dimensions as the old.

If adding a new faucet, just pull out the old sink with the faucet still attached. If you have plans for the old faucet, like recycling it, it's easier to remove the faucet from the sink after it's pulled out.

If you need to modify the sink cutout of your countertop, plan on a more time-consuming project, and be sure to buy a sink the same size or larger than your existing cutout.

Make sure you buy the right-size tailpiece, P-trap, and adapter that may be necessary to join the old stub-out. Bring the old drain pieces with you for size and overall setup and length.

With any sink, always read the manufacturer's installation instructions and safety precautions.

PREP WORK: REMOVE THE OLD SINK

- Clear away everything from under your sink for a clutter-free workspace.

- Set a flashlight in the cabinet and place a pillow or kneeling pad under you to work comfortably.

- If the faucet is mounted to the sink, unscrew the water lines from the shut-off valves, turn the water on at the faucet to relieve pressure and clear the lines.

- Under the countertop, check to see if there are any mounting clips holding the sink in place. If so, spray them with penetrating oil, and then unscrew them (a).

- From above the sink, you'll need to use a utility knife to cut through any silicone or caulk that has glued the sink to the vanity (b). Protect the countertop with cardboard if you're keeping it. With a utility knife, cut around the perimeter of the sink. If you need a more aggressive cutting tool, use a handsaw with a reciprocating blade.

- Disconnect the disposal if applicable (c).

- Unscrew the top nut on the P-trap to disconnect the tailpiece (d). If this nut won't budge, you may need to cut it out—with a reciprocating saw or close-quarter hacksaw, cut the old tailpiece above the P-trap. Remove the rest of the old P-trap and its tailpiece. (Be aware that mucky water will be in the P-trap.) With the P-trap removed, plug the stub-out with a rag (see the sidebar "Working with Drains and Traps" on page 121).

- You should now be able to pull out the old sink (e).

- Wipe away any old debris on the countertop with a scour pad if you're keeping it.

THE PROJECT

PREPARE THE CUTOUT IN THE COUNTERTOP

1 If your new sink is the same dimensions as your old, verify that it fits the same cutout and skip to Step 5.

2 If you're installing a new countertop or if your new sink has a different shape or is larger than the old cutout, you'll have to modify the existing hole. The sink should come with a cutout template. Center this template over the countertop as directed and trace the shape. Typically, a sink is centered to the countertop of the sink base cabinet—from side to side and back to front. If there is no template, turn the sink upside down, center it over the hole (if using the existing countertop), and trace the sink. Remove the sink, and trace another hole a ½ inch inside the one you just made—this will be your cut line.

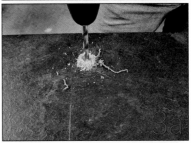

3 Use a drill bit to make a small starter hole for your jigsaw blade (a). The hole should be about an inch inside your cut line. Insert the jigsaw and cut around the entire cut line (b).

4 Test-fit the sink. Make any adjustments.

PREPARE THE SINK, FAUCET, DRAIN, AND TRAP

5 If your faucet mounts to the sink, follow the manufacturer's instructions and install it now, including the water supply lines (no-burst stainless steel recommended). Work with it on a padded surface (not visible in the illustration). If your faucet mounts to the vanity deck, install it now (see "Install a New Faucet" on page 105).

6 Put a bead of plumber's putty around the underside of the drain flange (strainer basket) and press it into the drain hole (a). Be sure to wipe away any excess that squeezes out. **Note:** If you have a double-bowl sink, this will entail mounting two strainers and connecting the drains accordingly. Double-bowl sink installation kits are available (b).

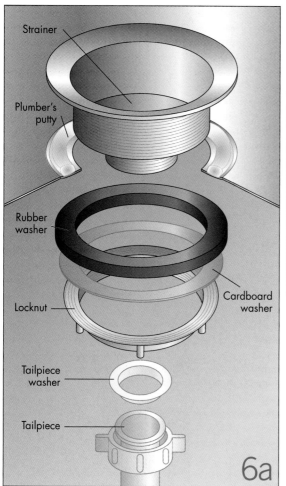

Strainer

Plumber's putty

Rubber washer

Locknut

Cardboard washer

Tailpiece washer

Tailpiece

6a

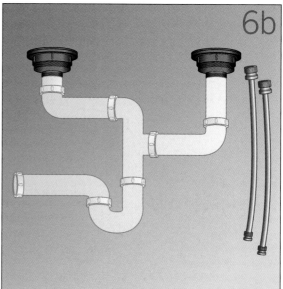

6b

7 Tighten the locknut, washer, and rubber gasket onto the basket (in that order), so that the rubber gasket tightens up against the sink. Use with tongue-and-groove pliers until the rubber gasket is snug up against the sink. Do not overtighten.

8 Insert the tailpiece washer on the tailpiece and tightening the slip nut, screw it to the bottom threads of the strainer basket.

9 With the sink still on its side or face down, apply a bead of silicone around the underside of the sink's rim.

DROP IN THE SINK AND HOOK UP THE FAUCET AND DRAIN

10 Carefully place the sink into the cutout, being sure it's centered. Press it down firmly and wipe away any excess silicone. Let it set.

11 Secure any mounting clips that may be provided to tighten the sink to the countertop.

12 Connect the water supply lines from the faucet to the shut-off valves.

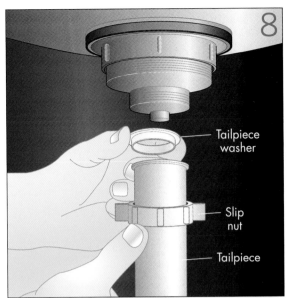

Tailpiece washer

Slip nut

Tailpiece

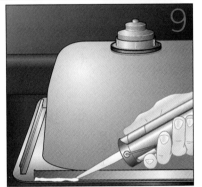

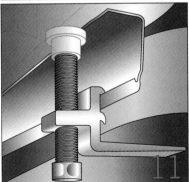

13 Test-fit the tailpiece, P-trap, and stub-out. You may need to add an adapter (a) or lengthen (b) or shorten (c) the tailpiece for the P-trap to meet the stub-out. See the sidebar "Working with Drains and Traps" on the next page. It may take a little back-and-forth to figure out proper alignment.

14 When the drain body, P-trap, and stub-out are all in place, slide down the slip-joint washers and nuts and hand-tighten them until snug.

15 Turn the water on at the shut-off valve and check for leaks.

16 Remove the aerator and turn on the faucet, testing the hot and cold.

17 Fill the sink with water. Check for leaks.

18 Reinstall the aerator, turn on the faucet, and check for leaks. Nice job!

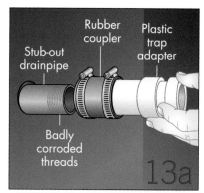

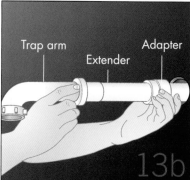

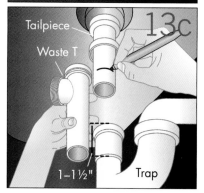

Working with Drains and Traps

Take a moment to check out your sink drain pipes. Basically, you'll see a pipe that has a deep curve in it—the P-trap (*P* because of its shape). The trap's purpose is to create a barrier between your home and sewer gases; it traps them through a water reservoir in that curve. Coincidentally, it will also trap your earring that falls down the drain, but that's not its intended purpose (although I'm grateful!).

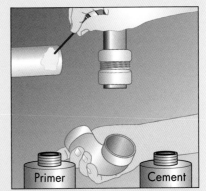

Old homes generally have galvanized drain pipes with brass fittings, while newer homes use PVC or ABS.

Changing out the old drain and trap is recommended if you're replacing your sink or faucet, especially if they're rusty or galvanized pipe. Take extra care when working with old and rusted pipes. They could break off unexpectedly while you're working on them. You'll want to cut out the old metal trap from the stub-out, because unscrewing it will be next to impossible. It's easiest to cut on the threads of the stub-out (the thinnest point). Use a reciprocating saw with a metal blade. This is not an easy cut if you're working under a cabinet and quarters are tight and awkward. Another option is to use a close-quarter hacksaw and a lot of elbow grease.

Once the old P-trap is removed, you'll need to clean the stub-out. Use an old knife to scrape away the built-up residue inside the pipe (it ain't pretty). This will help prevent future clogs. You

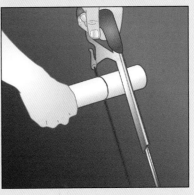

Primer   Cement

can now use a Fernco coupler (a short rubber section of pipe with clamps on each end) that will adapt the old galvanized stub-out to a P-trap.

PVC or ABS pipes are the easiest to work with. Slip-joint-type compression fittings on P-traps create a seal with a plastic washer (or ferrule) and nut. Simply slide the washer toward the pipe end and tighten the nut over the threads. No Teflon or pipe joint compound is necessary; however, threaded pipes that don't have this washer will need tape or glue around the threads when joined. These pipes use a primer and cement to join to one another where there aren't threaded fittings.

Often you'll need to cut or extend pipes so they align properly under the sink. You can cut them with a hacksaw or PVC cutters for PVC and ABS pipes. Know that a pipe should extend at least an inch past the washer to prevent leaks. Never force drain and trap parts together—if you do, they'll most likely end up leaking.

continued

If an off-center stub-out or an unruly drain setup is making you crazy, there are many options out there to make it right: flexible rubber or plastic traps, 45-degree and 90-degree angled elbows, adapters, and tailpiece extensions.

Kitchen pipes are typically 1½ inches in diameter, but this can vary. It's always best to bring old parts with you when shopping for proper size and overall drain setup.

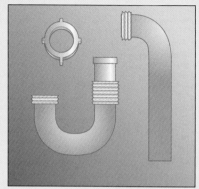

Flexible plastic trap

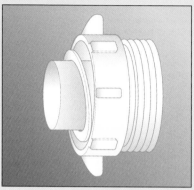

PVC reducer

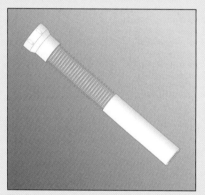

Flexible tailpiece extension

Countertops

In addition to a countertop's aesthetic appeal, you should also look for a durable surface that can withstand everyday wear and tear of kitchen life. Installing a great looking and hard-wearing countertop will make a huge impact on your kitchen's functionality.

Install a Laminate Countertop

WHAT YOU'LL NEED

Preformed countertop sections

Tongue-and-groove pliers

Drill/driver and various bits

Belt sander with 80-grit sandpaper

Scribing tool (compass with pencil)

26-inch-long crosscut handsaw with 8 or 10 teeth per inch or circular saw with thin kerf blade*

Hammer or rubber mallet

Pry bar*

Drywall saw*

Tape measure

Flashlight

Buildup strips

Framing square

Masking tape

End splash/end cap kit*

Household iron*

Contact cement*

Metal file

Miter bolts

Water-resistant wood glue

Metal L-brackets

1- to 1¼-inch wood drywall screws
(check the length of the screws so they won't puncture the laminate when driving through the bottom of the countertop)

Wood block

Putty knife

Joint compound

Caulking gun

Matching-color or clear caulking

* If applicable

A new countertop is a sure way to update the look of your kitchen. While you're at it, you should go ahead and put in a new sink and faucet for the full effect. You can order preformed countertops (also called post-formed) with a built-in backsplash from a supplier, and then do the installation yourself. The degree of difficulty for this project will vary according to how many turns the counter makes and how many walls it fits between, but with precise measurements, patience, and a little finessing, a new countertop is a weekend's worth of work away.

CONSIDER THIS: HOW TO ORDER YOUR COUNTERTOP

Precise measurements are crucial. Various suppliers ask for different specifications regarding measurements, so discuss measuring instructions with them in detail. Additionally, you should sketch a layout of your base cabinets and mark the exact width and depth of the cabinets. Also, mark where the walls, stove, sink, and refrigerator are located. The salesperson will use this information to calculate the right countertop size, including an overhang and surplus material that will be removed for a tight fit.

Even with the most accurate of measurements, sanding and cutting is normal. Walls are never perfectly plumb and square (hence, the finessing for a perfect fit). Use a framing square to check for straightness. If your walls and corners deviate more than ¼ inch, discuss this with the salesperson so she can account for even more material that can be scribed and cut away.

Counters with an inside corner should be ordered with precut miters. If applicable, be sure to order *buildup strips;* these strips are the height of the factory built-up edge under the front side of the countertop. Screwing them to the cabinet base tops will provide additional stability and support for the countertop.

If possible, order your countertop in one piece, eliminating the need to join mitered corners.

If you're replacing a backsplash, be prepared to do a wall repair if the new backsplash sits lower on the wall than the old one.

Countertops are heavy; it's best to work with a partner. Most damage caused to a countertop happens during installation. Work carefully and on a padded surface when applicable.

This project addresses the installation of an L-shaped, preformed countertop with a built-in backsplash and precut mitered corners—one length of the countertop is against a wall, and the other against an appliance, which makes this type of installation more involved than an open-ended straight run of countertop.

PREP WORK: REMOVE THE OLD COUNTERTOP

It's easiest to remove the sink and countertop all in one piece. You may disconnect them later for recycling or repurposing.

- Clear out everything from the inside the base cabinets and remove any drawers.

- Turn off the water at the shut-off valves.

- Set a flashlight in the cabinet for better visibility.

- Disconnect the water lines from the shut-offs.

- Disconnect and remove the P-trap from the faucet tailpiece and stub-out. Plug the waste line with a rag or cap.

- Cut through the silicone bead around the sink. Check to see if there are any fasteners under the sink holding it in place as well. Pry the sink up and out of the top (with the faucet still attached).

- Under the cabinet look for screws or fasteners holding the top to the cabinet base (a). Unscrew them all (b). If there are no screws, it may simply be held down with silicone—use a handsaw fitted with a 6-inch reciprocating metal blade to cut through the joint between the cabinet and top. If it's nailed down, use a pry bar to pry up the counter.

- Cut or pry the backsplash from the wall (if applicable).

- Lift off the countertop from the cabinet—this will be heavy, so work with a partner and be careful not to hurt your back.

THE PROJECT

1 If applicable, glue and screw the buildup strips along the top sides of the cabinet bases. Leave 1½ inches of space between the strips and the cabinet fronts. **Note:** The height of the buildup strips should equal the factory built up on the front side of the countertop (sometimes on the back as well).

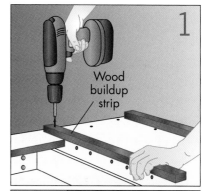

Wood buildup strip

2 Test-fit the largest section of countertop. It will probably (and intentionally) be too long. If this is the case, with a drywall saw, cut an opening into the wall that allows the corner of the miter to fit in it (so that the other straight side fits snugly against the opposing wall).

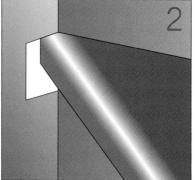

3 Measure how far the miter protrudes into the hole, and then subtract ¼ inch. Using a scribing tool set at that measurement, mark a line along the straight end of the countertop, running the tool the length of the wall (first wrap the end with masking tape). Scribing this way will mark the length needed for proper fit, as well as account for an unsquare corner.

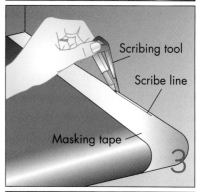

Scribing tool

Scribe line

Masking tape

4 Use a belt sander to sand away the surplus material on that end of the countertop until you reach the cut line. Test-fit the top and make sure the front overhang is parallel with the cabinet front. **Note:** Never let the belt sander run upward toward the laminate. This could cause the laminate to chip or pull away.

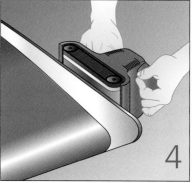

5 If the back wall isn't straight and prevents the countertop from creating a tight fit with the wall, it'll need to be scribed and cut. Place a strip of masking tape along the top of the backsplash. Run the scribing tool along the top of the backsplash (a). With a belt sander, sand to the scribe line (b).

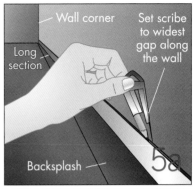

Wall corner   Set scribe to widest gap along the wall

Long section

Backsplash

5a

6 Test-fit the adjoining section of countertop, fitting it snugly against the one that's in place. Measure whatever space may exist that prevents the inside front corner of the mitered ends from fitting together.

7 Run masking tape along the back end of the backsplash, and using the measurement from Step 6, mark a scribe line down the entire length of the backsplash. Run the belt sander to remove material up to the scribe line.

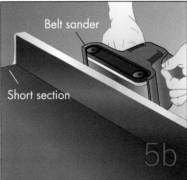

Belt sander

Short section

5b

8 Test-fit the counters again. They should fit snugly to one another as well as to the back walls.

9 Check the overhang on the open end of the counter. It may need to be cut flush with the cabinet if adjoining an appliance. Make this cut now—scribe a line on masking tape and cut with a circular saw (loaded with a thin kerf blade) or with a 26-inch-long crosscut handsaw with 8 or 10 teeth per inch. Leave the line as you cut, then fine-tune the cut with the belt sander.

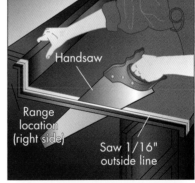

Handsaw

Range location (right side)

Saw 1/16" outside line

9

10 Finish the end with an end cap kit. Typically, laminate is glued to the end with contact adhesive or, if it's preglued, the heat from an iron activates the adhesive. Use a file to smooth the edges.

11 An end splash may require that an additional length of wood be glued and clamped to the edge of the countertop; then a matching laminate strip is adhered to the edge.

10

12 Temporarily connect the countertops with the miter bolts. There will be precut slots along the mitered sides made to receive the metal clamps of the bolt. Fit the bolts inside them and, with an open-ended wrench, screw them together loosely.

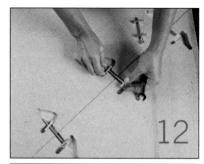

13 Spread water-resistant wood glue along both edges of the miter. Use a wood block and hammer to tap the joints flush with one another. Tighten the bolts, little by little, checking that the joint remains perfectly flat.

14 From beneath, screw the countertop to the cabinet. There are various ways to do this: You may use metal L-brackets, insert screws through the buildup strips (if they have predrilled holes), insert screws through corner cabinet brackets, or a combination of all the above.

15 Whatever you do, do not screw through the countertop and pierce the laminate. Check the length of the screw—it should sink approximately halfway through the countertop material, but no more than that.

16 Once the miter is dry, you may cut the opening to install your sink or range top. See the sidebar "Tips on Making Cutouts in Your Countertop" on the next page.

17 Use joint compound to close up the hole made in Step 2. Let dry and sand.

18 Making sure the backsplash is dust free, run a bead of silicone along the entire edge where the backsplash meets the wall.

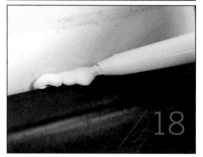

Tips on Making Cutouts in Your Countertop

The fixture or appliance maker will provide cutout instructions indicating the exact size of the cutout and where it should be placed. Usually a template is provided that you trace onto the countertop for exact measurements. Sometimes sink manufacturers instruct that you use the sink turned over as a template. Here are some tips to read before making any cutout

- Find the center of the cabinet base and mark it on the countertop—position the sink (or appliance) accordingly. Typically, a sink is centered to the countertop from side to side and back to front.
- Set the sink far enough back from the front of the cabinet so that it clears the framework of the cabinet.
- Apply masking tape all around the perimeter of the cutout area and trace the template line onto the tape. Typically, the cut line will be approximately a ½ inch inside the template line. Now trace the cutline.
- Masking tape should cover any surface that the base of the jigsaw may contact.
- In each corner, use a drill bit to make a starter hole for your jigsaw blade, and make the hole about an inch inside your cut line. Insert the jigsaw and start to cut the cut line. Use a fine-tooth standard jigsaw blade or special laminate cutting blade.
- If rounded corners are recommended, you may use a hole saw to bore out each corner and then a jigsaw on the straight cuts.
- Be sure to have someone prepared to catch the cutout as it falls away after it's cut.

Tile a Countertop

WHAT YOU'LL NEED

Tiles

Cap trim for backsplash

Trim for counter edge

Tongue and groove pliers

Flathead and Phillips screwdrivers

Palm sander or sanding block (120 grit)

Rubber mallet

Tile cutter

Tile file

Nippers

Notched trowel

Grout float

Drill bit slightly smaller than finishing nails

Drill/driver

Hammer

Nail punch

Miter box

Household detergent

Clean rags

Gloves

Safety glasses

Drop cloth or newspaper and painter's tap

Tape measure

Marker

Framing square

Stain/seal or paint that's washable and brush*

Latex modified thin-set mortar

Tile spacers*

Scrap of plywood

Scrap of a length of wood

Unsanded grout

Large man-made tile sponge

Continued on next page

A ceramic tile countertop is a classic choice for kitchens. Because of its durability, affordability (it may be even less expensive than laminate), and limitless style selections, no wonder it's such a favorite. Additionally, do-it-yourselfers thrive with all of the user friendly tile cutting tools on the market today—like a portable wet tile saw, which makes cutting numerous tiles a breeze.

CONSIDER THIS

- You will need to remove the kitchen sink for this project, which will involve additional plumbing steps if there's a dishwasher and/or food disposal present.

- It will take a few days to complete this project due to various drying times at different stages of the project.

- Know that tiles that are non-porous will perform far better as a countertop surface—fully glazed tiles work best. You may choose a porous tile, such as tumbled marble, but know that your countertop will need to be sealed periodically.

- Experiment with different sized tiles for countertop, backsplash, and trim (get samples from your tile store). You may find that a particular tile naturally fits a surface better than another.

- If the trim you choose for the counter edge (either tile or wood) has a right angle that sits on top of the counter, you must account for this lip when preparing the tile layout. You may choose to install this trim before laying the countertop tile. In this case, be sure that the trim is installed at a height that will be flush with the countertop edge.

- To calculate how much tile to purchase, determine square footage (length × width), then add 10 percent of that number to the total. Tile boxes will tell you the number of tiles and square footage it will cover.

- This project addresses tiling over an existing laminate countertop and backsplash. The backsplash and counter edge are trimmed with wood molding.

WHAT YOU'LL NEED

Continued from previous page
Bucket
Silicone caulk
Caulking gun
2-inch finishing nails
Wood clamps
Matching wood putty
* If applicable

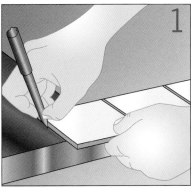

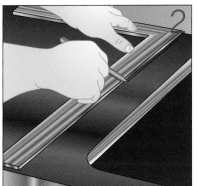

PREP WORK

- Clear away everything from the countertop. Unplug and remove all appliances.
- Place a drop cloth or tape newspaper on the floor surrounding the countertops.
- Inspect the existing countertop. Look for sections where the laminate has pulled away from the substrate. Carefully pry open the loose section with a putty knife (being careful not to crack it) and apply the contact cement following manufacturer's instructions.
- Remove the sink. Turn off the water at the shut-off valves, disconnect the water lines and trap, and remove the sink with the faucet still attached. (For detailed instructions on how to remove a sink, see "Install a New Drop-in Sink" on page 115).
- Sand down all the areas to be resurfaced, including any backsplash. This creates a tooth for the tile adhesive to stick to. You may sand by hand, or with a palm sander.
- Wash down all surfaces with a household detergent.
- When you're finished, the old laminate should be dry, dull, cleaned, and totally dust free.
- If you're using unfinished wood molding for trim, paint or stain/seal it now to allow for drying following manufacturer's instructions.

THE PROJECT

DETERMINE TILE LAYOUT

If you're tiling your countertop edges with special lipped edge tiles that fit over the top of the counter, (as opposed to finishing them with wood trim, as in this project, or using flat tile), you will need to use them when determining your layout and install them *first*, before the horizontal field tile. For more tips on installing a tiled edge, see the end of this project.

1 You will need to establish a starting course of tile. Line up tile in front of the sink so that the end tiles on either side of the sink are equal in size. Mark these points on the counter with a marker.

2 With a framing square, draw a line from the mark you've just made to the backsplash—do this on each side of the sink. These layout lines will establish your starting points, working out from the sink across the countertop.

3 Dry-fit a course of tiles along one of the layout lines. Use a length of wood to butt the edge tile against it to ensure proper line-up with the counter edge. If your tiles have tabs, cut them off with nippers. Then file smooth on one side of the edge tile (the side that will make a corner with the counter edge), so a tight corner joint will be created. Use tile spacers to account for grout lines if your tiles don't have tabs/nubs. If the tile that meets the backsplash needs to be cut to fit, take a measurement of the space, subtract an ⅛ inch and cut the tile to size. **Note:** Label the backs of cut tiles as you go to know exactly where they will be placed—for example, backsplash/left corner sink.

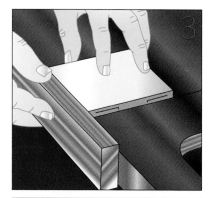

4 At the side of the sink, measure the space from the layout line to the sink opening (a). Cut the tiles to this size. For the tiles at each sink corner, hold a full tile over the corner and trace the opening on the back of the tile (b). Use nippers to cut away at the tile until you meet the cut line. If full tiles don't fit at the front of the sink, measure the space and cut the tiles to size. **Note:** For more tips on cutting tile, see "Tile a Backsplash" on the next page.

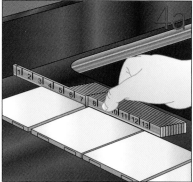

LAY THE TILE

5 After you've dry-fit all of the tiles surrounding the sink, you can begin laying tile. Apply mortar with a notched trowel around the sink opening as wide as one course of tile. Comb a uniform pattern of notches through the mortar about an ⅛-inch thick. **Note:** Do not spread more mortar than you are prepared to tile within 15 minutes. If the mortar starts to dry, scrape it off and reapply new mortar.

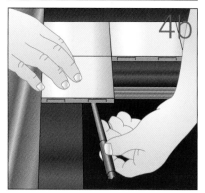

6 Begin laying tile at the corner of the sink. Use a scrap piece of wood against the counter edge to butt to the edge tile. Work your way up to the back splash and around the sink. As you lay the tile, press and twist them slightly into the mortar. Use tile spacers if your tiles don't have tabs. As you go, check that the tiles are all flush with one another.

7 After you've laid all of the tiles around the sink, spread more mortar a couple of courses wide out from one side of the sink. Lay the tiles, working from the edge back to the backsplash.

8 When you've laid a few rows of tile, use a square of plywood and rubber mallet to gently tap down the tile. Be sure to scrape away any mortar that may ooze out from between the tiles. Also, wipe away any mortar that may get on the face of the tiles with a damp rag.

9 Allow it to dry overnight, after the entire countertop surface is tiled.

TILE A BACKSPLASH

10 Line up the backsplash tiles to match the grout lines of the countertop. If the tiles need to be cut, take the measurement to the top of the backsplash, subtract an ⅛ inch and make your cuts.

11 Spread the mortar for a few tiles and press the tiles in the mortar. If the tiles are cut, put the cut side up. If the tiles don't have tabs, use spacers between the countertop and the tiles. If your backsplash requires more than one row of tiles, lay the bottom row first, then continue with the next row.

12 After several tiles have been laid across the backsplash, use the plywood and hammer to gently tap them in place.

13 Allow the backsplash to dry overnight.

GROUT THE TILE

14 Mix the grout according to manufacturer's instructions. Use a grout float to press the grout into the joints of the tile lines. It's best to hold the float at an angle and pass over the area firmly in a diagonal direction.

15 With a damp sponge gently wipe away the grout that remains on the face of the tile. Keep rinsing the sponge as you work.

16 Apply the grout to the entire countertop and backsplash.

17 As the grout dries a powdery residue will form. Gently wipe it away with a soft clean rag being careful not to wipe out any of the grout. Let the grout dry according to manufacturer's drying time.

18 When the grout is dry, wipe away any remaining powdery residue with a clean rag and apply the grout sealer according to manufacturer's instructions.

INSTALL THE TRIM

19 To cap the backsplash, measure and cut the lengths of trim you need. Make miter cuts for any inside corners using a miter box to cut the trim at a 45-degree angle. Test-fit the lengths and corners.

20 Apply a bead of silicone caulk along the back of the trim. Position the trim on top of the backsplash. Hammer the finish nails through the cap and into the backsplash every 12 inches, leaving them slightly above the trim. Use a nail punch to finish driving the nail slightly deeper than the trim.

21 Wipe away any silicone that may have oozed out.

22 Use a dab of matching wood putty to cover the nails, following manufacturer's instructions. **Note:** If using painted trim, allow the putty to dry, sand, then touch up with paint. The same will apply for the edge trim.

23 To finish the counter edge, measure and cut the lengths of trim. Make miter cuts for the inside and outside corners. Test-fit the lengths and corners.

24 Apply silicone to the counter edge.

25 Clamp the trim to the counter edge, making sure that the top of the trim is flush with the countertop. Wipe away any silicone that may have oozed out.

26 Drill pilot holes through the wood and into the counter edge approximately every 12 inches using a drill bit that is slightly smaller than the finish nails.

27 Hammer the finish nails into your pilot holes, leaving them slightly above the trim. Use a nail punch to finish driving the nail slightly deeper than the trim.

28 Wipe away any silicone that may have oozed out.

29

Use a dab of matching wood putty to cover the nails, following manufacturer's instructions.

If you're *tiling* the edges, consider these tips

- For the edge tile, you may use the same tile as on the countertop or special trim tile (for example bull nose tile or drip-edge tile). **Note:** Special edge tiles with a lip will need to be installed before the field tile.

- If using the same tile as the counter, they'll likely need to be cut—take the measurement of the edge, and cut the tiles to size. File the cut edge smooth. Install the finished edge facing up.

- Always be sure that the edge tile gives clearance to the drawers.

- Remove the top drawers and/or open the doors of the base cabinets to clamp a two-by-two to the face that will act as a ledger to support the edge tiles until they set.

- Before laying the tile, determine whether your grout lines for the edge will match exactly to the countertop or not. A near match will look like a mistake. In this case, experiment with lining up the edge tiles so the grout lines falls halfway between the countertop tiles. Start at the outside corner, placing the edge tile on the ledger for visual reference. See what layout will avoid having to cut tiny tiles. Experiment to see what layout works best.

- For **outside corners**, if using regular tile you can wrap the corner by having the front counter tile extend slightly past the corner in order to butt the side tile against it. Another option is to miter them. For special edge tiles, corner pieces are sold to fit outside corners—install them first, then fit the others.

- For **inside corners,** you can miter the tiles or butt them up to one another—grout will conceal the joint. If using special edge tiles, inside corner pieces are sometimes available.

Appliances

Some appliances require more than a plug-in the wall. The instructions for installing a dishwasher and microwave/exhaust fan are addressed in this chapter.

Install a Dishwasher

WHAT YOU'LL NEED

New dishwasher

Flathead and Phillips screwdrivers

Adjustable wrench

Drill/driver

Lineman's or slip-joint pliers

Wire nuts

Teflon tape

Dishwasher elbow

Stainless-steel braided dishwasher supply line

Drain hose

Drain hose clamp

Cable clamp (for BX cable or Romex)

Hanger or plumber's strapping

Non-contact voltage tester (pen-type)

Air gap*

Level

* If applicable

There are several great reasons to replace your dishwasher, but these days the obvious "out with the old, in with the new" holds far more meaning than just gaining a fresh new look. Purchasing an Energy Star dishwasher can save on your electric bill, in addition to saving hundreds of gallons of water each year. Because a dishwasher pulls both water and electric, choosing a high-efficiency one will help you go green for the environment *and* keep more green in your pocket—and there's never anything wrong with that.

CONSIDER THIS

It is important that you choose a dishwasher that fits in your dedicated base cabinet—typically 24 inches deep. Height on most dishwashers can be adjusted.

Both electric and water supplied to the dishwasher must be turned off for this project.

This project addresses removing an old dishwasher and replacing it with a new one—water supply, drain, and electric hookups are already in place.

Make sure you choose a dishwasher that's built in (for a base cabinet) and not convertible.

Check the owner's manual and installation instructions of your new dishwasher unit. Verify what water hookups it requires (for example, if the supply line connects to either the hot or cold water valve under the sink). Always follow the manufacturer's instructions and safety precautions.

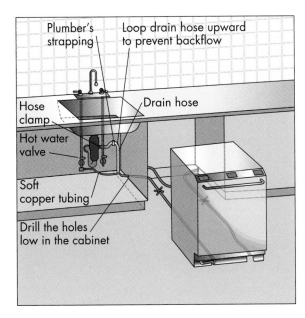

Plumber's strapping

Loop drain hose upward to prevent backflow

Hose clamp

Drain hose

Hot water valve

Soft copper tubing

Drill the holes low in the cabinet

PREP WORK: REMOVE THE OLD DISHWASHER

- Turn off the electric supply to the dishwasher from the service panel.

- Turn off the water at the shut-off valve that supplies the dishwasher (this could be either at the hot or cold valve under the kitchen sink).

- Remove the front panel on the bottom of the dishwasher (a) and locate the unit's junction box. Open the junction box to expose the wiring.

- Use a non-contact voltage tester to make sure that the power is indeed *off* (b).

- Unscrew the wire nuts and pull apart the green, white, and black wires. Recap the supply-line wires and lay it flat and out of the way.

- Locate the water supply line and disconnect it—have a flat pan and rag handy to catch any water in the line (c).

- Disconnect the drain hose from under the sink at the waste T or food disposal—loosen the clamp and pull it off.

- Open the dishwasher door and unscrew the two brackets that mount the dishwasher in place; they'll be located right in front, just under the countertop (d).

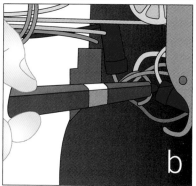

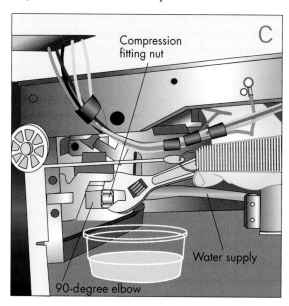

Compression fitting nut

c

90-degree elbow

Water supply

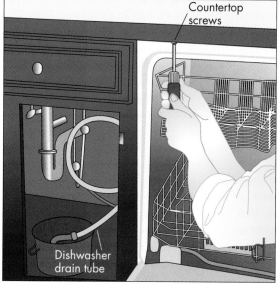

Countertop screws

Dishwasher drain tube

- Locate the adjustable legs and spin them with a wrench so they raise, which will lower the unit.

- Carefully pull the dishwasher out (e), being careful not to get caught in the electric or water lines or damage the floor. (You may want to put a large piece of cardboard or a blanket on the floor to protect it.)

- Unscrew the old water supply line from the shut-off valve and disconnect. Discard the old supply line. You may leave the old drain hose attached to the dishwasher to be discarded. The electric line may be reused.

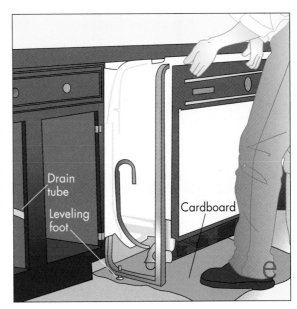

Drain tube

Leveling foot

Cardboard

THE PROJECT

Familiarize yourself with the manufacturer's instructions. They'll probably instruct you to remove or install certain articles immediately, like screwing on the adjustable legs or removing the toe-kick.

MAKE THE WATER SUPPLY AND DRAIN CONNECTIONS

1 Copper tubing with a compression fitting or braided stainless-steel dishwasher supply lines may be used to supply water from the shut-off valve to the dishwasher. I prefer braided lines—they're extremely durable, easy to install, and you never have to worry about kinking, denting, or splitting them, as you do with copper tubing.

2 Wrap Teflon tape clockwise around the threads of the shut-off and screw on the supply line—first hand-tighten it, and then give it a snug turn with a wrench. (Do not overtighten.)

3 Look to see which side of the dishwasher has the water hookup and electric hookup. The water and electric lines will run from the back of the appliance, on the floor, to the front hookups. Run the water supply line through the hole in the cabinet and position it on the floor. Have it follow a path that corresponds with a channel that is under the dishwasher that is provided to keep the supply lines cleared from the motor. Use painter's tape to secure it in position on the floor.

4 Manipulate the electric line so it follows a path that's cleared for its connection to the junction box. Tape it to the ground.

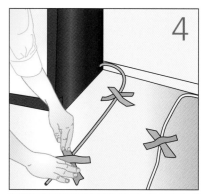

5 On a protected surface, gently tip the dishwasher onto its back. Wrap Teflon tape on the threads of the water inlet valve and screw on an elbow with a wrench—snug it tight.

6 Tilt the dishwasher upright and position it in front of the cabinet opening. Slip the hose clamp over the drain hose and slide it over the drain outlet on the back of the unit—tighten the clamp.

7 Guide the drain hose through the opening in the sink cabinet.

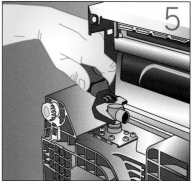

8 While kneeling down, gently push the dishwasher into its bay, holding it by its sides. Do not force the front panel, as this could damage the unit. As you push, guide the slack of the drain hose farther into the sink cabinet. Also, make sure that the water supply and electric line do not move as you're pushing. Make sure that none of the lines are kinked.

9 With the dishwasher in its bay, screw the water supply line to the elbow on the inlet valve—snug it tight with a wrench.

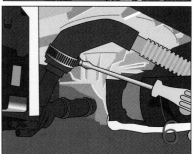

Honor Thy "Stemmie"

What the devil is a *Stemmie,* you ask? It's insider plumbing lingo for a person who is all-knowing, a master, a guru—simply put, a plumbing *god.* All the trades have their version of a Stemmie. If you're lucky enough to meet one, don't take it for granted—they're gems, I tell you! Once you get past their sometimes gruff exterior, they're more than eager to share their expertise with you. They have a wealth of knowledge—especially with the materials used in homes from your neighborhood for decades—that only time and experience can bring. You just can't get that from a book.

A Stemmie is often the grizzled-haired guy behind the counter of a parts shop. At a glance he can rattle off the brand, make, model number, features, benefits, and drawbacks of just about any old part you drop on his counter. I've learned so much from these guys—cousin Sal, Joe Barry, John, Wes, and, of course, the nationally renowned Bill "Stemmie" Harper. I've picked their brains about the how's and why's—hanging on every word.

So if you come across a Stemmie, I urge you to show him some love! Bring him a cup of coffee, give him a charming smile, tell him a racy joke. Trust me—when you're pulling your hair out because you can't figure out why that part you got from the home center won't thread right, you'll be so happy you did.

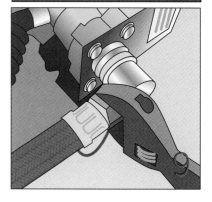

10 Connect the drain hose to the waste T from the faucet or to the food disposer. **Note:** In some places, local code requires that an air-gap system be present to prevent wastewater from back-flowing into the dishwasher (a). You can see the top of this device next to your faucet. If you have one, hook up the drain hose to the inlet tube of the air-gap. Another hose will run from the discharge tube to the food disposal or waste T (b). I recommend that you change this unit when installing your new dishwasher. Replace it following the manufacturer's instructions.

11 Unless you have an air gap (see Step 10), it will be necessary to run the drain hose in a high upside-down U shape, secured to the back or cabinet wall, and then into the waste T or food disposal.

12 Raise the drain hose up at least 32 inches from the floor and screw it in place using the provided hanger or plumber's strapping. Be careful not to puncture the hose while screwing.

13 Wrap Teflon tape to the threads and screw the water supply line to the shut-off valve.

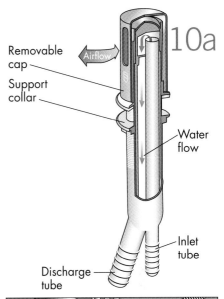

10a

Removable cap

Airflow

Support collar

Water flow

Inlet tube

Discharge tube

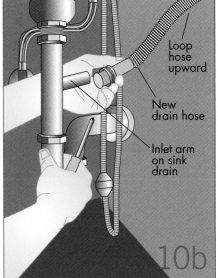

Loop hose upward

New drain hose

Inlet arm on sink drain

10b

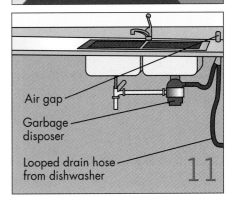

Air gap

Garbage disposer

Looped drain hose from dishwasher

11

MOUNT THE DISHWASHER IN ITS BAY

14 Open the dishwasher door and hold a torpedo level to the top of the unit. Level as necessary, spinning the legs to adjust height. Check for level from side to side and back to front. If you need to adjust a rear leg, you may need to loosen the electric box to gain access to it.

15 Most manufacturers require a clearance of ½ inch from the countertop bottom to the top of the unit—adjust accordingly.

16 Fasten the mounting brackets that secure the unit to the countertop.

MAKE THE FINAL ELECTRICAL CONNECTION

17 Whether your electric supply line is metal (BX cable) or plastic sheathed (Romex), you must first clamp it to the junction box of the dishwasher. Bundle the wires and slide a clamp onto the cable until just the loose wires are exposed.

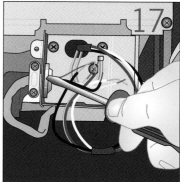

18 Unscrew the starlike nut from inside the junction box, insert the clamped wires, and tighten the nut so it's snug against the wall of the box.

19 With wire nuts, connect the white to white, black to black, and green to green (or bare copper wire). If you have BX cable, wrap the dishwasher's ground wire (green or bare copper) around the screw that's located in the wall of the junction box—the metal armor clamped to the box acts as a ground in this instance.

20 Screw the cover plate onto the junction box.

21 Restore power and water to the unit.

22 Turn on the dishwasher and check for leaks at each connection.

23 Install the cover panel.

Install a Microwave/Exhaust Fan

WHAT YOU'LL NEED

New over-the-range microwave with mounting hardware

Tin snips*

Hammer

Screwdrivers

Nail set

Stud-finder

Tape measure

Pencil

Level

Safety glasses

Ducting*

Duct tape

* If applicable

Over-the-range microwaves are an effective way to save counter space. They also offer lighting and venting, making this multipurpose appliance one of the most functional units in your kitchen. The thing is, when one function goes, you pretty much have to replace the whole thing. The upside is, in one installation you've got yourself three brand-new features.

CONSIDER THIS

A microwave is heavy. It's best to work with a partner unless you have the strength of Hercules . . . and four arms.

It's crucial to have proper measurements when choosing your microwave.

The unit *must* be anchored into wall studs. Some manufacturers require fastening into at least one stud.

This project addresses installing a plug-in, over-the-range microwave that is externally vented with a top exhaust.

Always follow the manufacturer's instructions and safety precautions.

PREP WORK

- Unplug the unit.

- Disconnect the ducting. Remove the duct tape—a utility knife will help. See if there is a small screw securing the exhaust adapter to the straight duct—if so, unscrew it to pull them apart.

- If your unit is totally kaput and you're going to junk it anyway, with it *unplugged,* cut the cord—this will prevent the cord from getting caught up as you're hoisting the microwave out.

16 ⅛"
30"
30" min.
2"
66" min.
Backsplash

- There are several different ways your old unit may be mounted. Open the top cabinet and check for screws or bolts on the bottom shelf. Remove the front grille and check for long screws that extend to the back of the unit. There may be a sleeve that holds the microwave in place; this will need to be removed as well. It will take some investigating, but eventually all the mounting hardware needs to be removed.

- When dismounting the unit, proceed with caution. Be prepared for the unit to fall at any moment. It's always best to work with a partner.

THE PROJECT

CONFIRM VENTING CONFIGURATION AND PREPARE THE MOUNTING SPACE

1 Familiarize yourself with all the parts and hardware that came with your unit.

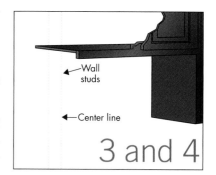

2 Check to see if the unit has come assembled in the venting configuration that you need. If it hasn't, follow the manufacturer's instructions on adapting the unit to meet your ventilation type— either recirculating (ductless), outside top exhaust (vertical duct), or outside back exhaust (horizontal duct). You may also need to redirect the blower unit to adapt to your venting setup.

3 Find the center of the space between the cabinets and mark a center line with a level.

4 Locate the studs—this may be evident from the way in which the preexisting bracket was mounted. Mark the studs on the wall with a level.

MOUNT THE HANGING BRACKET TO THE REAR WALL

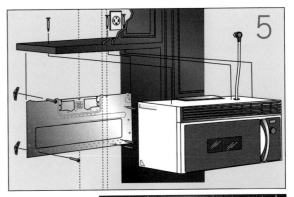

5 Screw the mounting bracket (plate) to the wall. It is imperative that one of the brackets is screwed directly into a stud. Some units have a cross bracket that stretches the span of the opening. If neither side of the bracket hits a stud, this cross bracket will have several holes in it that will certainly accommodate one stud. In this case, center and hold the mounting bracket in the opening and with a pencil, mark your screw holes

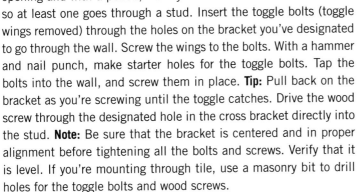

so at least one goes through a stud. Insert the toggle bolts (toggle wings removed) through the holes on the bracket you've designated to go through the wall. Screw the wings to the bolts. With a hammer and nail punch, make starter holes for the toggle bolts. Tap the bolts into the wall, and screw them in place. **Tip:** Pull back on the bracket as you're screwing until the toggle catches. Drive the wood screw through the designated hole in the cross bracket directly into the stud. **Note:** Be sure that the bracket is centered and in proper alignment before tightening all the bolts and screws. Verify that it is level. If you're mounting through tile, use a masonry bit to drill holes for the toggle bolts and wood screws.

PREPARE THE TOP CABINET

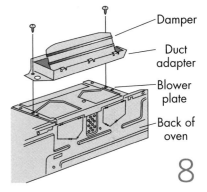

Damper

Duct adapter

Blower plate

Back of oven

6 Some units provide a template that is used for the precise marking of holes needed to mount the unit into the top cabinet. (Templates are sometimes provided for marking the rear wall as well.) Tape the template to the bottom of the top cabinet as directed by the manufacturer.

7 Drill holes with the indicated bit size. Be sure to wear safety glasses when drilling overhead.

PREPARE AND MOUNT THE MICROWAVE

8 Check that the damper moves freely. Be sure to remove any tape or packing materials. Mount the damper and duct adapter to the microwave.

9 Check to see how the house duct will fit over the damper/adapter. If your house duct is not the same shape or size as the adapter on your unit, you'll need a special transition adapter—such as a rectangular-to-round. Test-fit it over your unit's adapter. You may need to make some adjustments to the damper to ensure that it still pivots freely when installed.

10 Make sure that any contents in the microwave have been removed.

11 With a partner, raise the unit into the space. Feed the cord into the allotted hole in the cabinet. You may need to first catch the bottom of the unit onto a lip of the bracket, and then tilt it under the cabinet. Never raise the unit by its handle or with the door open.

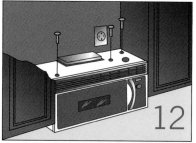

12 While one person holds the unit against the rear wall, the other should fasten the designated screws through the bottom of the shelf of the cabinet into the aligning holes of the unit. Thread all the screws just until they catch. Tighten the center screw first, and then tighten down the rest.

CONNECT THE DUCTWORK AND FINISH INSTALLATION

13 Slide the house duct into/over the adapter or transition adapter.

14 Wrap duct tape around each connection. Be sure that every joint is thoroughly sealed.

15 Plug in the unit.

16 Install the grease filter(s).

17 Turn on the unit and check that it's operating properly.

Cabinets

Cabinets make a significant impact on the look and feel of your kitchen. They can also ward off ensuing arguments . . . like one regarding the 162 piece plastic food storage set you picked up at the local club store that your spouse told you, you didn't need and have no place to put, anyway. (Uh, yes, I absolutely do need them, and I have plenty of room to store them.) Replacing your cabinets will update the entire look of your kitchen as well as give you the opportunity to install upgraded drawer and shelf systems for hassle-free and spacious organizing.

Install New Cabinets

WHAT YOU'LL NEED

New cabinets

Tongue-and-groove pliers

Pry bar

Hammer

Screwdrivers

Drill/driver

Countersink bit (3/16-inch)

Miter box

Circular saw

Block plane

Utility knife

Ladder

4-foot level

Stud-finder

Pencil

Tape measure

2½-inch wood screws

Cabinet washers

1½-inch pan-head screws

C-clamps (Quick Grips, preferably)

Wood shims

Masking tape

Finish nails

Filler strips

Molding

Toe-kick trim

Nothing makes more of an impact on a kitchen than new cabinets. Similarly, no project will make you want to pull your hair out quite the way hanging cabinets will. What makes it so daunting is getting them to all line up perfectly straight—straight meaning level, square, and plumb. While you may have these principles straight in your head, invariably, your floor and walls will not. However, when they're finally installed, visual satisfaction paired with an amazing sense of accomplishment will make you stand back, look at your kitchen, and say, "Wow, this looks amazing, and I did it myself!"

CONSIDER THIS

The most important detail to get you started on this project is proper layout. You can't be exacting enough with measurements to ensure that your cabinets fit your space precisely how you intend them to. When ordering cabinets, working with a kitchen design pro is a huge help. She'll provide you with a floor plan of where each cabinet will go, making installation much easier. Be sure to bring a detailed sketch of your kitchen that not only indicates floor, wall, and ceiling dimensions, but the placement of sink, stove, refrigerator, windows, and so on.

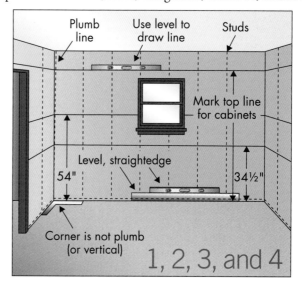

Be prepared to have your kitchen out of commission for the duration of this project. Set up a makeshift kitchen in another section of your house, with a coffeemaker and microwave, to get you through the project.

Water and gas will need to be turned off in your kitchen.

Removing the old cabinets is a major project in and of itself. Prepare an area to store your dishes, pots, small appliances, and so on.

It's best to work with a partner for this project, especially when hanging wall cabinets.

This project covers removing old cabinets and installing new ones that will work with the existing plumbing, electric, and gas lines. If you're changing the layout of your kitchen, once the old cabinets are removed and the new layout is established, all the utility lines should be set up at this point.

Any painting or new flooring is ideally done after the old cabinets are removed and before the new ones are installed.

If you'll be installing a vented exhaust through the cabinet above the range, know the dimension of the opening and make the cut before installing the cabinet.

PREP WORK

- Clear out everything from the cabinets and countertops. Remove all drawers and shelves.

- If possible, remove the stove and refrigerator from the space. If you have gas, turn it off at the valve behind the stove and unscrew the supply line.

- Turn off the water from the shut-off valves and disconnect the water lines to the faucet and P-trap to the sink.

- Remove the sink (see "Install a New Drop-in Sink" on page 115).

- Remove the countertops (see "Install a Laminate Countertop" on page 124).

- Remove the base cabinets. Look for screws or nails that secure them into the walls. Use a pry bar if necessary. Work carefully to avoid damaging the walls. If possible, it's easier to pull out the cabinets in one unit, while they're still screwed to one another. You can dismantle them once they're removed.

- Remove the wall cabinets. Follow the same steps as above.

- Verify that you've received the correct cabinets. Assemble the cabinets if necessary, but do not install the doors. If the doors have come installed, remove them, but be sure to keep track of which door belongs to which cabinet.

THE PROJECT

PREPARE THE WALLS FOR INSTALLATION

1 Locate the studs with a stud-finder. With a level, mark vertical lines around the room indicating the studs. **Note:** The most accurate way to mark a stud is to run the stud-finder along the wall in one direction. It'll beep when it hits the edge of the stud—make a mark. Then run it along the wall in the other direction, marking the other edge of the stud. Draw two vertical lines at these marks. The space between them represents the stud.

ESTABLISH WALL CABINET HEIGHT

2 Pick a wall where cabinets will be hung. At any point from the floor measure up the wall 54 inches—make a small pencil mark. With a 4-foot level, use that mark to draw a horizontal line around the room. This line will establish an initial base point. **Note:** Normally, 54 inches allows for a 36-inch base cabinet and countertop, plus 18 inches of space between the countertop and the bottom of the wall cabinet. If your cabinet configuration requires a different wall cabinet height, measure accordingly.

3 Take measurements around the room, every couple of feet, measuring up the wall 54 inches and making small pencil marks. Because the floor probably isn't level, invariably some 54-inch marks will fall above this horizontal line. This indicates high spots of the floor. The mark that falls highest above your initial base line will be the correct height to mount a ledger. Use that mark to draw a new horizontal line around the room.

ESTABLISH BASE CABINET HEIGHT

4 Repeat Steps 2–3, but this time mark 34½ inches—the standard height of base cabinets.

5 Using the lines you've marked on the walls as reference, draw the layout of each cabinet on the wall. Be sure to mark the front-frame measurement of the cabinet, which is the actual size. (Sometimes the back of the cabinet is smaller than the face frame.)

HANG WALL CABINETS

6 Mounting a ledger facilitates hanging the wall cabinets in two ways: It establishes the proper height and steadies the cabinet when it's being screwed in place. With finish nails or screws, fasten one-by-threes into the studs at the exact height of the horizontal level line (aligning the *top* of the one-by-threes with the level line). Do not sink the nails or screws through the one-by-threes so you can pull them out easily after the wall cabinets are installed.

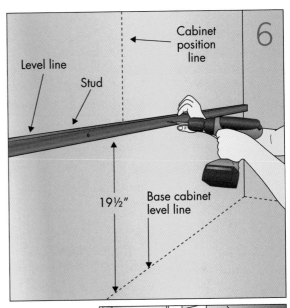

7 Starting from one end of a wall, or an inside corner if there is one, from the edge of that cabinet drawing, measure the distance where the studs align on that cabinet. These measurements must be transferred to the back of the cabinet.

8 From the edge of the actual cabinet, use a level to transfer the stud measurements to the cabinet back.

9 Drill two small holes through the hang rails of the cabinet at each stud point, about a ¾ inch from the top and ¾ inch from the bottom. (Use a ³⁄₁₆ countersink drill bit.)

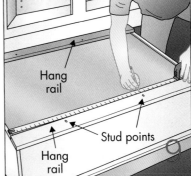

10 Raise the cabinet onto the ledger and screw the cabinet in place using 2½-inch deck screws with cabinet washers. Do not tighten them down completely.

11 Hang the adjoining cabinet following Steps 6–9. **Note:** You may realize that a smaller cabinet may fall *between* studs. If this is the case, drill holes for toggle bolts and mount accordingly.

12 Clamp the mating cabinets together by their vertical stiles, making sure the face frames are flush with one another. Be sure they're clamped together good and tight. Just below the top hinge and just above the bottom hinge, drill pilot holes and screw the two cabinets together. Be sure that your screw length penetrates straight through one stile and halfway through the adjoining one. If there is no face frame, screw through the cabinets near the hinges.

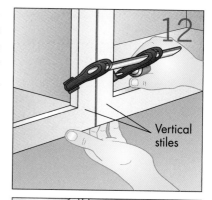

Vertical stiles

13 Repeat Steps 7–12 for the entire run of cabinets.

14 Once all the cabinets are secured to one another, place shims wherever gaps are created between the wall and the backs of the cabinets. Screw the shim locations through the hang rails inside the cabinet. With a utility knife, cut and then crack the excess shim sections that protrude from the cabinets.

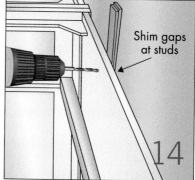

Shim gaps at studs

15 Now that the cabinets are screwed together and shimmed, tighten down the screws that secure the cabinets into the studs.

INSTALL BASE CABINETS

16 It's typically easier to secure two base cabinets to one another first, and then install them as one unit. On a piece of plywood (or a flat surface), working with the cabinets on their *backs*, fasten adjoining cabinets to one another following Steps 7–12. Once the fronts are screwed together, true them up to one another (that is, make sure the front measurement of the cabinets are the same as the back). With the cabinets now upright, take measurements at the face of the cabinet and at the back—they should be equal. Shim as needed so that they're the same measurement in the front, middle, and back—screw them together right through the shims.

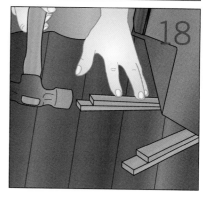

17 Carefully lift the unit and place it against the wall.

18 Where needed, use shims under the cabinets to raise them uniformly up to the horizontal level line.

19 Now that the cabinets are level, secure them to the wall. **Note:** On both wall and base cabinet, filler strips may be needed to fill in spaces due to odd dimensions or to allow clearance for doors and drawers to operate properly. They should be fastened to the face frame, through the stile of the adjoining cabinet in the same fashion in which cabinets are joined together. When they're against walls, they can't be clamped. Slightly overcutting them, and then planing or sanding them down to size will offer a tight fit. To cut filler strips, measure the gap where the filler strip will go at the top and bottom of the adjoining cabinet, and add 1/16 inch to each measurement. With a straightedge, transfer the cut line (on masking tape) to the back of the strip. Set the circular saw at a 10-degree bevel, and with the strip clamped down, make the cut so the wide side of the bevel remains on the front side of the strip.

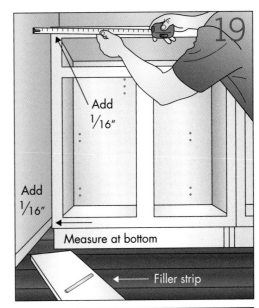

Add 1/16"

Add 1/16"

Measure at bottom

← Filler strip

FINISH INSTALLATION

20 Trim molding is used to finish cabinetry when cabinets meet an adjacent wall, soffit, ceiling, or any place unfinished edges are left exposed after installation. Toe-kick trim (matching wooden pieces made to conceal the shims under the cabinets) should be installed at this point as well—quarter round or vinyl molding may be used as well (a). Use a miter box to make 45-degree cuts for corner joints. Nail the trim to the face front or exposed back edge of a cabinet with small finish nails (b).

21 Hang the doors with provided hinges. Use the adjustment slots in the hinges to raise or lower the doors so they line up with one another.

22 Install the drawers and shelves.

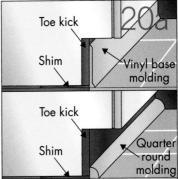

Toe kick

Shim

Vinyl base molding

20a

Toe kick

Shim

Quarter round molding

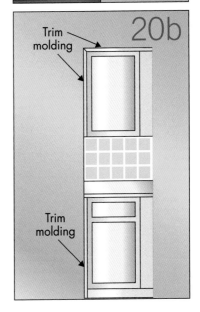

Trim molding

20b

Trim molding

Under-cabinet Lighting—A Bright Idea

Under-cabinet lights are excellent for task and accent illumination. I especially like the puck-style ones because they remind me of cute little mini high hats made specifically for cabinets. Kits are available that make installing them a cinch.

Plug-in units are the real no-brainer. You can attach them directly to the bottom of the cabinet, or drill holes to make them recessed. The wire simply runs through small holes drilled in the sides of the cabinet, plugs into an outlet, and is controlled with a roll switch on the wire. Some are remote controlled, so a wall switch can be mounted anywhere you choose.

A hard-wire unit is ideal to install when you're hanging new cabinets. After the old cabinets are removed, tap power from a nearby outlet, pull wires through the wall studs at an appropriate height behind the cabinets, and then feed the wire through the cabinets as they're being mounted into position. Wall repairs are easily hidden behind the new cabinets. For steps on how to pull wires, see "Install Recessed Lights" on page 166.

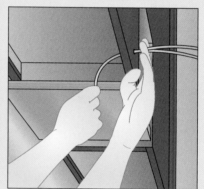

Walls and Floors

Imagine walking to your kitchen entry . . . *click* . . . on go your newly installed can lights . . . then *Wow!* . . . as you gaze down to see how beautifully they illuminate your brand new floor. Now if that's not a reason to do your best Fred Astaire across the room, around the center island, and over to your refrigerator, I don't know what is.

Install a Floating Floor

WHAT YOU'LL NEED

Pre-glued floating floor planks

Flush-cut saw

Jigsaw

Circular saw or hand saw

Hammer

Steel pull bar

Utility knife

Large and small banger blocks

Underlayment

Masking tape or duct tape

Tape measure

Speed square

Pencil

Floor manufacturer sealant or 100% mildew-resistant silicone

Caulking gun

Baseboards and show molding*

Miter box

Doorway/floor transition*

* If applicable

I've fantasized about a floating floor . . . like when someone is droning on and on about some painfully inane subject—I sit patiently, listening and nodding, but all I'm wishing is that the floor would pick me up and float me the hell out of there. Now that's a floor!

I've exposed my daydream vision of a floating floor, but the actual meaning of one can evoke dreams of the home improvement kind . . . like when you've installed the last plank of your beautiful new floating floor knowing that you'll never have to stare down at the crusty old carpet again. *Aaah . . . now that's a floor!*

A floating floor is actually an installation system as opposed to a type of flooring material. Using this method, planks are installed by snapping or gluing them together. They aren't nailed or glued to a subfloor, so they float, expanding and contracting with humidity as one entity. These floors have grown in popularity, especially in the do-it-yourself market, because of their affordability and ease of installation. They're also available in materials such as laminate and engineered hardwood, making selections vast and versatile.

CONSIDER THIS

A floating floor can be installed over almost any type of existing floor: concrete, vinyl, ceramic tile, and so on. What's imperative is that the floor be stable and level.

Everything possible should be removed from the kitchen floor, including the refrigerator and stove.

To calculate how much flooring to purchase, determine square footage (length × width), and then add 10 percent of that number to the total. The flooring box will tell you the number of planks and square footage it covers.

Buying planks that are preglued is a great timesaver.

Decide whether you want to remove your old baseboards and replace them over the new floor, or leave them in place and nail shoe molding to them in order to cover up the expansion gaps.

A doorway or floor transition may be necessary to mate two floors of different heights. Consider the flooring of the adjoining room and purchase the appropriate transition.

The boxes of flooring must stay at room temperature 48 hours prior to installation.

The instructions for this project are to install a preglued engineered wood floating floor over a plywood subfloor.

Always follow the manufacturer's directions and safety precautions.

PREP WORK

- Bring the boxes of flooring into the room and allow them to acclimate to room temperature for 48 hours.

- Clear everything from the kitchen floor.

- Examine the floor to see if any sections are loose. If, say, a vinyl sheeting seam is coming up, nail it down with flooring nails. If a section of tile is missing, use concrete patch to fill it in.

- Pry off the existing molding if installing it over the new floor.

THE PROJECT

PREPARE THE FLOOR

1 The door casing and jambs will need to be cut in order to fit a plank. To calculate the height that needs to be cut, stack a piece of underlayment and plank (back side up, not to damage the plank), and hold it up to the bottom of the casing. With a flush-cut saw, cut through the casing and jamb on both sides of the doorway.

2 Vacuum the entire floor to prepare it for the underlayment. This foam cushion will minimize minor floor irregularities and provide sound dampening.

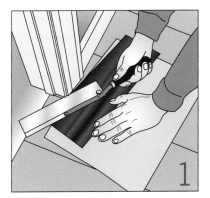

3 The underlayment should go down perpendicular to the direction of the planks (typically, planks run parallel with the longest wall). Roll sections of foam underlayment over the entire floor and cut it to fit with a utility knife. Seal the joints with duct tape or masking tape. Be sure not to overlap the underlayment.

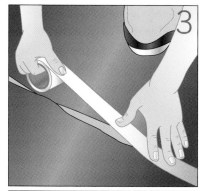

PLAN THE FLOOR LAYOUT

4 Planks typically run parallel with the longest wall. The entire perimeter of the floor must have a small expansion gap of approximately a ½ inch to allow the planks to expand and contract with humidity—check the manufacturer's specification for spacing. Before getting started you need to determine how wide the last course of planks will need to be. It's likely that last course of planks will need to be ripped to size (a cut made down the length of the plank).

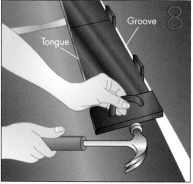

5 To calculate this measurement, measure the room's width in inches, and then subtract 1 inch for the expansion gaps. Divide that number by the width of one full plank. If you find you're left with a number resulting in a plank that's more than 1½ inches, you're good to go. But if that last course is less than 1½ inches, resulting in a scrawny sized plank, you'll need to rip the first course of tiles so the last course will be wider.

6 Similarly, if the length of the first course of planks leaves you with a stubby end plank, you'll need to cut the first one so the last will be longer. Calculate as stated above.

LAY DOWN THE FLOORING

7 In a corner of the room, place spacers against the starting walls and set down the first plank with the grooved end facing the wall. The tongues on the planks should always face out toward the room.

8 Join the next plank to the first. Use a hammer and banger block to tap and snap the tongue into the groove of the first plank. **Note:** Some planks are harder to join than others. You may need to hit the banger block forcefully and several times along the length of the plank. For the planks to be joined properly, the tongue must disappear completely into the groove. Continue laying planks in this manner, remembering to place spacers along the wall as you go.

9 To place the last plank of the course, hold it up to the wall, and with a spacer set against the wall, take a measurement remembering to subtract a ½ inch for the expansion gap (a). Mark the plank with a straightedge and cut the plank to size using a hand saw, jigsaw, or circular saw (b). To install the last plank, you can use a pull bar to insert it into the adjoining plank. **Note:** Using a pull bar gives you the means to tap the planks together when the proximity of the wall stops you from being able to swing the hammer.

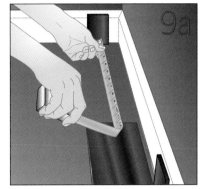

10 To start the next course, keep in mind that you must stagger the planks so joints won't fall in line with one another. You can use the remainder of the plank you cut from the prior course, but only if it's an ample length, typically 8 inches or more. Continue laying the planks in this manner.

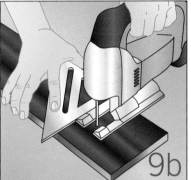

11 Notch planks as needed to accommodate doorways and cabinets. Be sure to leave a ½ inch for the expansion gap.

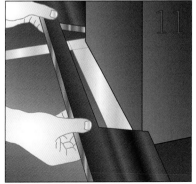

12 When you reach the last two courses, use a pull bar and hammer to tap the planks into position.

13 After the floor is down, use the manufacturer's sealant or 100% mildew-resistant silicone to seal the expansion gaps. Check the manufacturer's installation instructions to see exactly where they specify sealing the floor, but typically it's around the refrigerator, sink, and dishwasher. Allow the sealant to dry before installing baseboards or shoe molding.

14 To conceal the expansion gap, nail baseboards to the walls with finish nails. Do not put nails through the flooring. For corners, cut 45-degree angles. To join molding in a long run, make a scarf joint, cutting the ends at 30-degree angles; this makes a seamless-looking joint as opposed to butting the molding end to end. **Note:** It's easier to paint molding before installing it.

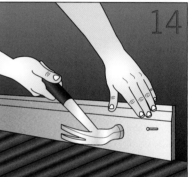

15 If part of the expansion gap is still exposed, you may use ¼-inch round shoe molding to finish the edge. Again, nail it to the baseboard and not to the floor.

16 If applicable, cut the prefinished doorway/floor transition to size, and snap, nail, or glue it in place.

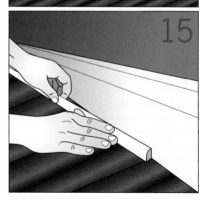

Tile a Floor

WHAT YOU'LL NEED

Floor tiles

Screwdriver

Rod saw

Nippers

Manual or wet blade tile cutter

Drill/driver

Noncorrosive countersinking screws

Utility knife

Floor scraper

Metal putty knife

Heat gun*

Rag

Tape measure

Pencil and marker

Cement backer board (¼ inch)

Backer-board cutter

Carpenter's square (or framing square)

Thin-set mortar

Notched trowel

Tile spacers

Furring strips

Compass*

Cardboard*

Earplugs

Mask

Safety glasses

Alkali-resistant fiberglass tape

4-foot level

Abrasion stone

Grouting supplies—matching grout, bucket, grout float, large man-made sponge

Grout sealer

Threshold transition

* If applicable

Tile floors are a favorite for kitchens because of their durability and ease to keep clean. They don't absorb odor or water, making spills worry free. They always offer an impressive upgrade to a kitchen and will instantly transform the entire look of the space. Today, do-it-yourselfers thrive with user-friendly tile-cutting tools on the market—like a portable wet tile saw—which make cutting numerous tiles a breeze.

CONSIDER THIS

To achieve a successful tile job, you must have a sound subfloor and underlayment. Any unstable or uneven surface will ruin a new tile installation.

Everything possible should be removed from the kitchen floor, including the refrigerator and stove.

Generally it takes 24 hours before you can walk on newly installed tile. Check the adhesive manufacturer's instructions and drying times.

Be sure to choose tiles that are specifically made for floors (typically wall tile is not dense enough to hold up as flooring).

To calculate how much tile to purchase, determine square footage (length × width), and then add 10 percent of that number to the total. Tile boxes will tell you the number of tiles and square footage it will cover.

You'll need to choose a threshold that will transition your kitchen tile to whatever type of flooring is on the other side of the door. The threshold could be wood or marble, but, most important, it must be able to accommodate the two types of flooring.

This project addresses removing a deteriorating vinyl tile floor from a plywood subfloor, installing a ¼-inch cement backer-board underlayment, and then laying ceramic tile.

PREP WORK

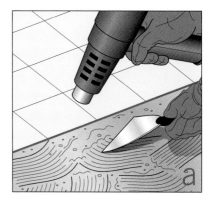

- Remove everything possible from the kitchen floor.

- Remove any shoe molding. (If there is only baseboard, plan to add shoe molding to create a finished look.)

- Remove the old vinyl tile using a floor scraper. For stubborn tile, a heat gun is useful to loosen the adhesive (a).

- Make sure that the plywood subfloor is sound and flat. Replace any damaged sections.

- Clean away all loose debris.

THE PROJECT

INSTALL ¼-INCH CEMENT BACKER BOARD

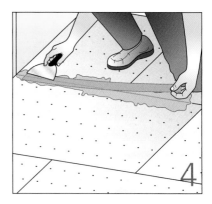

1 Determine the layout of the cement board—aligning the boards perpendicular to the subfloor joints. Be sure to stagger all the joints. Allow a ⅛-inch gap between board edges, walls, and cabinets. Score and snap boards as you would drywall.

2 Trowel a ¼-inch layer of modified thin-set onto the subfloor. Embed the boards into the wet mortar.

3 Screw the boards in place every 8 inches with appropriate screws. Be sure the screws are flush with the surface. Do not fasten screws ⅜ inch from board edges or 2 inches from the corner to avoid cracking.

4 Prefill joints with the same thin-set, and then embed alkali-resistant fiberglass tape and smooth down and seal the joints with an additional pass of mortar. Allow the mortar to dry completely before tiling.

DETERMINE CERAMIC TILE LAYOUT

5 You'll need to establish a starting course of tile. Between the two most prominent walls, dry-fit tiles using spacers. Your goal is to end up with the following criteria for optimum results.

- Full tiles at the doorway
- Equal-size tiles along the walls that face one another
- No sliver-size tiles—avoid a layout that creates a course of tiles that need to be smaller than 2 inches

You probably won't be able to achieve all these criteria, so you'll need to make choices. Keep in mind the big picture of the floor. For example, tiles running along the toe-kick of a cabinet base aren't very noticeable.

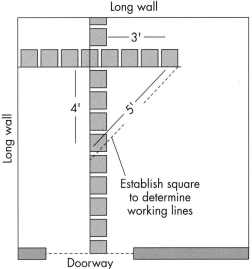

Long wall

Long wall

3'

4'

5

Establish square
to determine
working lines

Doorway

5, 6, and 8

6 Once the first course of tiles is determined, dry-fit a second perpendicular course at the center of this row. See if this produces an acceptable layout according to the criteria listed above—adjust one or both of the rows if necessary.

7 Line up a carpenter's square on top of one corner of the tile intersection; mark a right angle on the floor. Remove the tiles.

8 To establish your working lines, use one leg of the marked right angle to snap a chalk line from one wall to the other. Snap a second line to the opposite walls using the other leg of the right angle. Check for square using the 3-4-5 method; see the sidebar on page 165. (This step is particularly important for larger floors where going even slightly off square will be cumulative over long courses, resulting in a sloppy-looking tile job.)

9 Because it'll be hard to see the chalk line as you apply the mortar, screw down two straightedges (one-by furring strips work well) that will act as guidelines, creating a quadrant to tile in. Put painter's tape on their edges to prevent mortar from sticking to them.

LAY THE TILE

10 Apply mortar with a notched trowel in a square slightly larger than a few rows of tile.

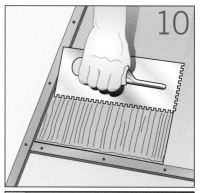

11 First, use the straightedge to lay out the tiles, and then use the tile edges to continue keeping uniform joints.

- Be sure to use tile spacers in between each tile unless tiles have built-in nubs.
- Use the butt of your palm to embed tiles in the mortar.
- Slide a bedding block over tile and tap with hammer or mallet.
- Check for plane regularly with a level.
- If a tile sinks, pry it up and add mortar beneath it.
- Clean out any mortar that may squeeze up through the joints.
- Keep using the carpenter's square to check that your rows are square.

Continue to lay out all the full tiles (also called *field tiles*) in this quadrant. We'll leave all cut tiles for the end.

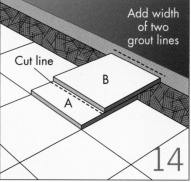

12 Unscrew the straightedges and rescrew one of them along one of the remaining chalk lines. Continue to spread mortar and lay all full tiles in this section.

13 Repeat the above step with the remaining chalk line until all the full tiles are set.

14 Once the full tiles are dry, come back and lay all the cut tiles.

- To cut a **straight border** tile, do the following to transfer the border measurement onto the tile: Lay a tile exactly over the adjoining full tile (tile A). Lay another tile over that tile, but line it up so that it rests over the border space leaving a width of two joints away from the wall or cabinet (tile B). Use this tile to mark a line across the tile beneath it. Take the marked tile and cut it.
- To cut an **outside corner,** follow the preceding step twice—once on each side of the corner. This will create an L shape to be cut out that will fit that corner perfectly.
- Cut all of the border tiles in a run first, number them (in case the wall or cabinet isn't square), and then lay them in that order. Always do a dry-fit first.
- For **odd-shaped cuts,** use a compass to transfer the shape onto the tile, or use cardboard to cut a template, and then trace the shape onto the tile.

More Tile Tips

- Use a rod saw and nippers for curves and small cuts. Make the larger cuts first, and then finer cuts with these tools.

- If the rod saw doesn't fit in the opening that needs to be cut, unscrew one side of the blade, fit it in the opening, and then refasten the blade.

- Don't let mortar sit for more than 10 minutes without laying tile on it. If it starts to dry, scrape it off and reapply.

- If you finish a section, scrape away any remaining mortar.

- Do not walk on tile for 24 hours after it has been installed.

- Avoid heavy traffic on the floor for 72 hours after tile installation.

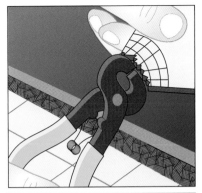

15 Once all the tile is dry, grout the entire floor (for grouting tips, see "Tile a Backsplash," on page 74).

16 After the grout has dried for 48–72 hours, seal the grout joints with a penetrating sealer. Follow the manufacturer's instructions and safety precautions.

17 Replace molding or install shoe molding, and install the transition.

Establishing "Square" with the 3-4-5 Triangle Method

This method is used when needing to establish a right angle from two lines. The rule is, if you measure out 3 feet on one line, and then 4 feet on the other, the diagonal line that would join those two points will equal 5 feet, but only when that angle is at exactly 90 degrees.

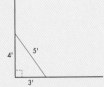

When using this method, you'll mark 3 feet and 4 feet on the given lines, and then adjust the angle they create, checking to see when you hit a 5-foot diagonal.

This method is best performed by two people, each using a tape measure to layout the two lines with a third tape measure to check for the 5-foot diagonal. Just be sure you're both measuring from the same side of the tape measure or the measurements will be off by the width of the tape. Once square is established, chalk lines may be snapped to create accurate working lines.

If we're going to get technical, it's actually the *Pythagorean theorem*—$a^2 + b^2 = c^2$, where *a* and *b* are the sides creating the right angle, and *c* is the diagonal line facing the right angle (a.k.a., the *hypotenuse*). (In this case, $3^2 + 4^2 = 5^2$, or $9 + 16 = 25$.)

Who knew back in high school that you'd end up using all that seemingly useless math to lay tile in your kitchen?

Install Recessed Lights

WHAT YOU'LL NEED

Remodel can kit

Downlight or eyeball lights

Appropriate bulbs

Drywall saw

Flathead and Phillips screwdrivers

Lineman's pliers

Metal cable cutters*

Ladder

Non-contact voltage tester (pen type)

Dropcloth

Stud-finder

Pencil

Graph paper

Tape measure

Safety glasses

Electrician snake (fish tape reel)

Electrical tape

BX cable (metal armored cable) **or Romex** (plastic insulated cable)—**wire gauge according to high-hat manufacturer**

Wire strippers

Utility knife

Wire nuts

Cable clamps or connectors

Coated staples

Bucket

Plaster of Paris

Joint compound

Putty knife

Sandpaper

* If applicable

Recessed lights (also called cans, high hats, downlights, eyeball lights, and so on) create a seamless look to a ceiling. Their unobtrusive characteristic allows them to integrate with practically any décor or ancillary light source. Some types are directional, making them an ideal task light for countertop work areas or a sink.

In a new construction, recessed lights are installed to the joists and wired before the ceiling goes up. Happily there are types designed for remodel construction (cut-in cans) that are installed through an existing ceiling. While holes still need to be made to run wiring, they're minimal and easily repaired with a simple drywall patch. Of course, if you have access to above your kitchen ceiling, like through an attic, cans can readily be installed and wired without making additional holes . . . or the need for red-ruffled skirts and folksy French music. Sorry, I couldn't resist a can-can joke.

CONSIDER THIS

Installing cans requires an ample comfort level of working with electrical projects.

If you discover your wiring is aluminum (dull gray in color) as opposed to copper (dull orange), call in a pro.

Power to the fixture you'll be working from must be turned off from the service panel before starting this project.

This project addresses replacing a surface-mounted light fixture and installing five recessed lights using retro-fit (remodel) cans with plastic insulated cable (Romex)—the ceiling is drywall and there in no access from above it.

If you install high hats in a ceiling where insulation is present, be sure to purchase ones that are rated for this application.

Know that there are two parts to a high hat—the housing can and the light. The light can be the fixed downward type, or directional eyeball type.

Be sure to purchase bulbs that are suited for your particular high hats.

It's always best to hire a licensed electrician to inspect your work before restoring power.

PREP WORK

TO FIND THE CIRCUIT AND VERIFY THAT IT CAN HANDLE ADDITIONAL LIGHTS WITHOUT OVERLOADING

- You'll first need to isolate which breaker controls the light fixture in your kitchen. To do this, turn on the lights in all the rooms. Start flipping breakers. When the kitchen light goes out, see which others have as well.

- Count how many fixtures are on the breaker. To speak in general terms: If your circuit is a 15 amp, the total wattage on that circuit cannot exceed 1,250 watts. Count each fixture in that circuit as 100 watts. With that wattage number in mind, see if adding your desired number of high hats will exceed that amount. If so, reduce the number of high hats you were planning to install or call in a pro to run a new circuit.

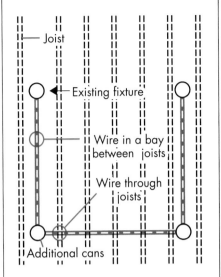

a

TO MAKE A CEILING PLAN

- Locate your ceiling joists and determine what direction they're running along the ceiling and how far apart they are from one another (typically 16, 18, or 24 inches).

- Draw a sketch of your ceiling indicating joist placement, where your existing fixture is, cabinets, appliances, sink, and where you'd like to add the recessed lights. Know that in the ceiling, at the can locations, you must have clearance from beams, pipes, ducts, or any obstruction. Cans come in different sizes, requiring that you make different-size holes—take this into consideration when drawing your plan (a).

You must also verify the height clearance in the ceiling; it should be about 8 inches. If it's not, you must purchase smaller high hats that require less space to install. To check height clearance, tap a small nail hole through the ceiling and insert a wire hanger—see how far it goes up until hitting the subfloor of the room above.

Note: In this project, the existing fixture will be changed to a high hat. Know that it is illegal and dangerous to enclose/bury a junction box behind a wall. If your existing fixture does not fit into your layout, you must blank it out—cover the box with a decorative plate that conceals it, but still provides access to it. Another option is to install a ceiling fan or coordinating fixture in its place.

- Put down a dropcloth under the work area.

THE PROJECT

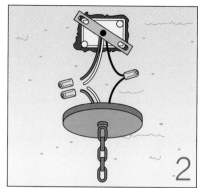

CUT THE HOLES

1 With the power off to the fixture (from the main panel and the switch), use a non-contact voltage tester to make sure that the power is, indeed, off.

2 Remove the existing light fixture (see "Install a Task Light Fixture" on page 92).

3 Disconnect the wires from the junction box.

4 Examine how the junction box is mounted in the ceiling. It may be screwed to a beam, or braced between beams with a hanging bracket. Unscrew and remove the box as needed.

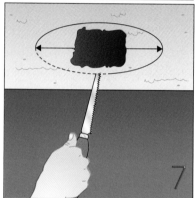

5 Use the template that came with your high-hat kit and trace it around the existing opening.

6 Before cutting out the hole, drive a nail in the center of it and insert an L-shaped piece of hanger wire. Swing it around to verify that there are no unforeseen obstructions.

7 Use a drywall saw to cut out the opening. Be sure not to cut outside the line.

8 Using the template, measure and trace the other circles onto the ceiling according to your layout.

9 Cut out those holes.

RUN THE WIRES

10 Measure and cut lengths of cable that will run between cans, adding a couple of feet of slack for each fixture.

11 If your cans run parallel to joists (straight through a bay), simply snake the wire from the existing fixture hole to the next one closest to it. Let the wire dangle from the hole.

To snake wire: Feed the tip of the snake from one opening to the next. When it reaches the second opening, pull it out and tape the cable to the tip of the snake with electric tape. Pull the snake out from the first opening, which will bring the cable along with it. If the wire has to traverse a joist, cut a small rectangular slot in the drywall under the closest beam to the can—removing a small piece of drywall under the beam itself and a couple of inches on each side of it (a). Run the wire from the existing fixture, drop it down on one side of the beam, pull it up through the ceiling from the hole on the other side of the beam, and then run it to the high-hat hole (b).

12 Repeat these steps until each can has cable running to it.

CONNECT THE WIRING

13 Open the plate on the junction box of the high hat and separate the wires. Pry out one of the metal knockouts on the box and insert the cable wire into the box, and tighten down the clamps.

14 With lineman's pliers, twist together the wires from the power source with the wire from the cable you've run for the closest high hat—black to black, white to white, ground (green) to ground (bare).

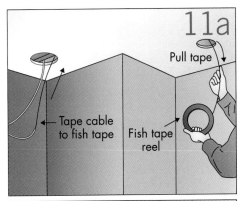

11a

Pull tape

Tape cable to fish tape · Fish tape reel

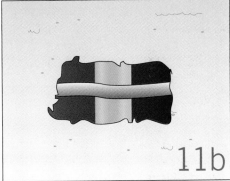

11b

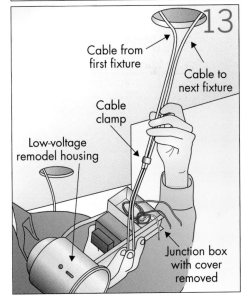

13

Cable from first fixture

Cable to next fixture

Cable clamp

Low-voltage remodel housing

Junction box with cover removed

15 Strip the stranded wires from the high hat to expose a couple of inches of wire.

16 Take the twisted white cable ends and wrap the stranded wire from the high hat around it. Take a wire nut and screw it onto these three wires; it should be snug. Repeat this step for the black and the ground. Fold all the wires into the box and close it. Let the fixture hang from the ceiling, and move onto the next one.

17 Cut the plastic sheathing on the cables for the next high hat a few inches. Insert them in the box through the knockouts and tighten them down. Connect all the wires as described in Step 14.

18 Continue these steps until all the high hats have been wired.

MOUNT THE HIGH HATS IN THE CEILING

19 Leading with the box, guide the high hat into the ceiling. Feed the cable slack into the ceiling as you raise the housing (or can). Raise it until the can is flush with the ceiling.

20 Use a screwdriver to flip the mounting clips until they're tightened against the ceiling.

21 Move on to the next can. Pull the cable slack up into the ceiling of the next can, and mount it as directed in Steps 19 and 20.

22 Once all the cans are mounted in the ceiling, push any remaining cable up into the ceiling, being sure that the cable left outside the ceiling runs flat on the bottom of the joist (if crossing a joist).

23 Use plastic-coated staples to nail the cables to the bottom of the beams. Make sure they're as flat as possible. Be careful not to puncture the sheathing.

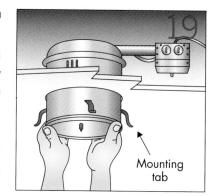

Mounting
tab

23

24 Install the light baffles and trim as directed by the manufacturer's instructions.

25 Screw in all the bulbs and restore power. Flip the switch on and check that they're all working.

PATCH THE HOLES

26 In a bucket, make a mixture of plaster of Paris following the manufacturer's directions. Working quickly with a putty knife, mix the plaster with an equal amount of joint compound.

27 Use the putty knife to spread this mixture over the holes to bury the cable. Fill in the cutout completely. Let it dry.

28 Make another pass with joint compound to fill in imperfections if necessary. Let it dry.

29 Sand the patch smooth. Prime and paint.

Slot for spring

Mounting spring

Innter baffle

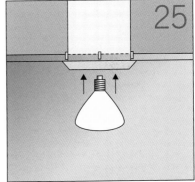

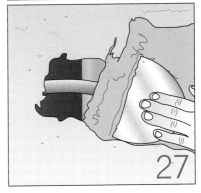

Part 4

Total Indulgence: Dreaming Up the Perfect Kitchen

Footprint and Layout:

What Works for You

A well-appointed and properly laid out space is the foundation upon which you'll build your dream kitchen.

Exploring the Possibilities

It strikes me funny to think that at one time the concept of "kitchen" was a fire built on the ground in the middle of a dwelling space. Something so basic—a place to cook food—that fulfills our most primordial necessity—eating—has turned into a multi-billion dollar industry spanning the realms of invention, engineering, and interior design. Kitchen remodels can be the most costly renovation in a home. There is so much to consider when embarking on a kitchen renovation and mistakes can cripple both time and budget—not to mention being out of a place to prepare a meal for what will seem like an eternity. When choosing cabinetry, appliances, and fixtures, taking the time to do your homework is crucial for a successful remodel. In addition to the aforementioned, one must carefully consider layout and footprint.

Layout describes placement of cabinets, appliances, and fixtures, while *footprint* describes the configuration of the walls that surround them.

No matter what the size or shape of your kitchen, there are three principles that must always be considered when designing a kitchen.

- **Inherent space characteristics**—Some examples of these characteristics would be window placement, ceiling height, soffits, radiator, and so on.

- **Standardized space guidelines**—These measurements were established to ensure a person's comfort and safety when performing all kitchen functions. Space guidelines exist for every room in a house. Always check local building codes before planning a remodel.

- **Flow and Functionality**—These elements speak to how the entire space moves and performs relative to each element. For example, does the refrigerator door block a passage to a busy part of the kitchen when it's open? Is there adequate prep surface near the sink and stove?

The best way to experiment with layout is to sketch the space on graph paper, using each square to represent a unit of measurement—say each square equals 3 inches, so 4 squares equal a foot. Be sure to mark not only existing room dimensions, but all fixtures and features of the space—door swing, windows, outlets, and so on.

Now ask yourself, what works in the space, what doesn't? Where are the traffic jams? What are the inconveniences? Think about kitchens you've been in that have really rocked your world: What was it about them that made navigating in them such a pleasure?

Survey what rooms share common walls to the kitchen and consider where logical footprint changes can be made. For example, does the existing space allotted for the refrigerator back up to the wall of a closet? That would offer a perfect opportunity to bump the refrigerator into that space, opening up more room in the kitchen, with minimal effect on the adjoining room.

Always keep in mind that bigger is not necessarily better. Sometimes "big" will just translate into time-consuming added steps in getting from point A to point B, with no real payoff. A small, well-appointed space will always be more enjoyable to use than one that is uselessly large.

The Work Triangle and Basic Layouts

One of the first things to consider when remodeling a kitchen is the *work triangle*. An invisible design pattern, the work triangle addresses a kitchen's three major work stations—the sink, stove, and refrigerator—and how efficiently they relate to one another. An ideal work triangle makes navigating between these elements effortless. (I've been in some kitchens where the work triangle feels more like the Bermuda Triangle— turbulent, mysterious, with reported disappearances of spatulas and flying soufflé pans.) It's important to realize that the tighter the triangle, the more quickly you can navigate from each station. At the same time, a triangle that's too compact can feel cramped and leave little space for prep surfaces.

The National Kitchen & Bath Association has developed distances between these points that optimize the functionality and flow between these three elements. Keep in mind that these distances are just guidelines and are not compulsory for a kitchen to function well. (I designed a kitchen in my New York studio with a layout that would have puzzled a few geometric physicists, but it worked given the inherent characteristics of a limited amount of space.)

NKBA recommends the following work triangle guidelines:

- The sum of the three work station distances should total no more than 26 feet with no single leg of the triangle measuring less than 4 feet nor more than 9 feet.

- Distances are measured from the center-front of the sink, stove, and refrigerator.

- No leg of the work triangle should intersect any other appliance, island/peninsula, or other obstacle by more than 12 inches.

With the work triangle in mind, you can explore layout options. The following represent some standard kitchen layouts.

- **L-shape**—One of the most common layouts, the L-shape makes optimal use of a space by incorporating a corner in the plan. Using the corner increases storage and countertop space. An ideal work triangle may easily be achieved with this shape. One drawback is that corner counter and cabinet space may be difficult to reach. In a larger kitchen you can build a *double L-shape* where a smaller L-shaped island is incorporated within the space. This layout can provide abundant work and storage space, even seating. (See "Island," below.)

- **U-shape**—Using three walls, this shape provides ample storage and countertop space. Typically, one of the three work stations will be placed on each wall. Because of its open design, there's less opportunity for traffic interference in the work triangle. However, this plan is not ideal for entertaining because all work stations face a wall. To function optimally this plan needs a minimum of an 8-foot-by-8-foot room to accommodate the recommended 4 feet of workspace from the center point of the room.

- **Island**—This design works best in larger kitchens where navigating around the island will not interfere with a major traffic path or work triangle. The island can provide a place for a rangetop, sink, or simply a prep surface. Seating may also be created on one side of the island. The length and placement of the island must be considered in order not to intersect a functional work triangle.

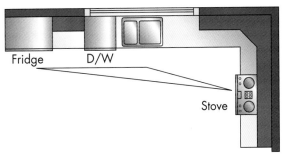

L-shaped layout with work triangle

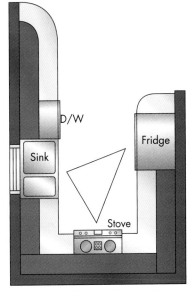

U-shaped layout with work triangle

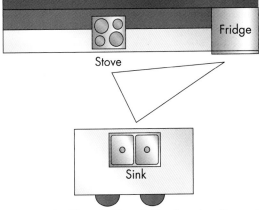

Island layout with work triangle and seating area

- **Peninsula (G-shape)**—This layout offers the opportunity to create a breakfast bar or entertaining space on the open leg (peninsula) of cabinetry. For proper seating, the countertop should overhang the base by at least 9 inches for leg room. Storage is also possible above and below the peninsula.

- **Galley (or corridor)**—Mostly found in smaller kitchens, this layout's greatest advantage is minimal movement for the cook because it creates a highly efficient work triangle. Obviously, cramped prep surfaces can be an issue, but for a limited space it's the most functional design.

- **One wall**—For a long and narrow kitchen, this layout is pretty much your only option. While you can't create a triangle from a straight line, you can situate the three work stations in a way that optimizes functionality. Ideally, the refrigerator should be on the far end (with the door swing away from the leg) and the stove on the other. The sink should be in the middle with 4 feet of counter space on each side of it.

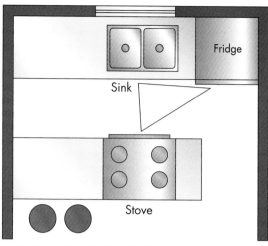

Peninsula layout with work triangle and seating area

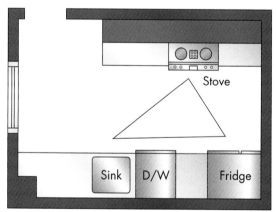

Gallery (or corridor) layout with work triangle

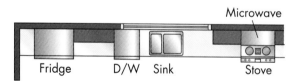

One wall layout with sink in the center

Consider This for Kitchen Layout and Footprint

Once you've contemplated workstations and basic layout and have sketched the kitchen on graph paper (see the "Exploring the Possibilities" section on page 175 for sketching details), do the following.

- Pencil in arrows on the page to show movement in the space from the entry to each work station, especially to the refrigerator and sink where there's the highest traffic. Ask yourself questions like, "Will I have to keep moving out of the way of the stove when my kids keep raiding the fridge?"

- How important is it to you to have a kitchen that is ideal for entertaining? Or are you the kind of chef who likes privacy while you're creating meals? Do you enjoy having your kids or someone help you with food prep? Examine your kitchen lifestyle before making any layout decisions.

- Never underestimate the necessity for counter space; it seems like there is never enough. Always seek to increase counter space whenever possible. When space is limited, installing a folding leaf to a countertop is ideal when cooking for large gatherings. A rolling kitchen island with a butcher block top is another convenient way to create an additional working station. When it's not needed, just tuck it against a wall and out of your way.

- In addition to providing a work station (sink or stove) and seating, islands offer incredible extra storage space. Appliances such as dishwashers and trash compactors may also be placed in an island as well as garbage and recycling bins.

- Never forget to account for where you are going to place your garbage and recycling bins. It may sound silly to mention, but I lived in a house where the only possible place to keep a garbage receptacle was on the opposite end of where the sink was located. Every time I needed to clear scraps from plates or throw away food packaging or cuttings, I had to hike all the way over to the entry of the kitchen—which, in addition, didn't make for a lovely first glimpse of the kitchen, a garbage pail. Whether they're tucked away in or next to a cabinet, make sure that they are conveniently and even aesthetically positioned.

Creating Storage Space

Insufficient storage is probably the number one complaint regarding kitchens (all around the home for that matter—give me more closets!). Small kitchens pose inherent space limitations, but large kitchens, if not well appointed, can present storage issues as well. Blenders, food processors, mixers, juicers, toasters, toaster ovens, pots, pans, and so on—where will they all go? Relying on countertops to store occasionally used small appliances can block work space as well as make the kitchen look cluttered and untidy. Happily there are several ways to create efficient storage space, no matter what the size of your kitchen.

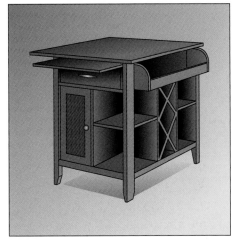

An island with a wine rack provides a creative storage space.

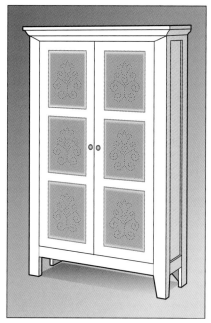

A pie safe offers extra storage as well as a design element.

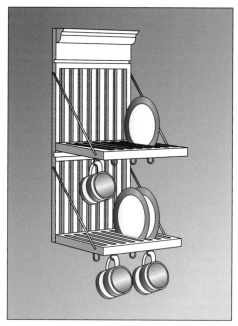

A hanging dish rack frees up counter space around the sink.

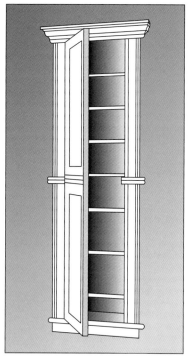

A recessed wall cabinet adds storage without taking up room space.

A cabinet with a pop-up shelf acts as an ideal storage and work surface.

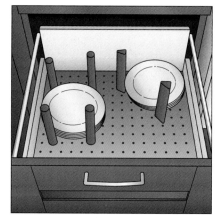

A Pegboard drawer holds articles in their place.

Storage Space for Medium to Large Kitchens

- Use a corner of the room to build a pantry with its door catty-corner to the kitchen. Run electric to the space for lighting: A door light switch that trips on the light each time the door opens is extremely useful. Have shelving built in against the walls in a catty-corner design as well so that there are three sides to it.

- Islands are a great way to get creative with storage. An aesthetically pleasing wine rack, shelves for decorative fruit and bread bins, as well as drawers and cabinets are just some of the ways to add storage with an island. A hanging pot rack above the island will free up cabinet space as well. Use your imagination . . . .

- A distinctive stand-alone piece of furniture, like a cupboard or pie safe, adds storage space as well as an interesting design element.

- A wine bar cabinet and hutch can be used to store everything drink related. I also like the idea of setting this up as a drink station for parties to keep the other work stations of the kitchen free.

Storage Space for Small Kitchens

- Install wall cabinets that go all the way up to the ceiling to maximize storage.

- A window does not need to be wasted wall space. Install a dish rack in front of one— it will free up cabinet space and still allow light to pass through.

- Install recessed wall cabinets. Although they will be shallow, they're perfect for storing glasses, bottles, cans, jars, and cereal and pasta boxes without taking up the space that a pantry or cabinet would.

- Hang a dish rack above the sink to free up counter space.

- Install a cabinet with a pop-up shelf that can hold a small appliance for immediate use.

Consider This for Storage

- Even with additional storage, organizing the space within it can present its challenges. Using shelf- and drawer-organizing systems will help keep order in these spaces. For example, a Pegboard-lined drawer with strategically placed dowels will keep articles in their place.

- Base cabinets with sliding shelves can make looking for items less time-consuming (and less back breaking!).

- Be sure to keep a stepladder or footstool nearby to reach high shelves and cabinets.

- Keep frequently used items in easy-to-access places—infrequently used ones, up and out of the way.

- For deep base, wall, or corner cabinets, a Lazy Susan is ideal to access articles.

Wheelchair-Accessible Kitchen

Barrier-free design, which supports accessible living for individuals with disabilities, has given rise to a broader approach of space solutions called *universal design.* This concept embraces all people. "Handicap" design meant sterile, institutionalized-looking amenities, which is far too unappealing and stigmatizing. Happily, universal design has embraced the notion that good looks matter just as much as functionality.

Whether it's adults planning for a senior parent to move in, or individuals anticipating recovering from surgery, trends show people are more eager to opt for many universal design options when making kitchen layout decisions.

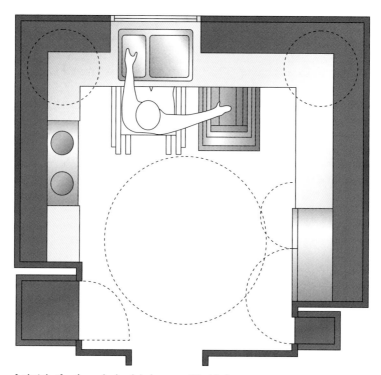

A sketch of universal wheelchair-accessible kitchen

The Layout and Work Triangle for Universal Design

As with standard kitchens, the layout and work triangle are crucial when designing an efficient wheelchair-accessible kitchen. Keeping the sink, refrigerator, and stove as close as possible puts less burden on the cook. Review all of the following elements and decide on a layout that fits the needs of the individual as well as corresponds with the characteristics and limitations of the space.

MANEUVERABILITY

- It's imperative for an area of the kitchen to be large enough for the wheelchair to turn around. If this is simply not possible because of space constraints, an area just outside of the kitchen should be cleared for this purpose.
- For a complete 360-degree turn, there needs to be a 5-feet-by-5-feet cleared space.
- In smaller kitchens, a T-turn (three-point turn) may be achieved by providing a minimum 3-feet-wide knee space opening under one of the countertops, where a point of the turn would be achieved by rotating under this counter space.

COUNTERS

- Create uninterrupted lengths of countertops so an individual can slide articles from place to place. An L- or U-shaped layout works best for continuity of surface, whereas a galley/corridor layout is less effective. A single wall layout may also work well by keeping the three stations close, making it less tiring for the individual to work in that space.
- Countertop heights should be between 29–34 inches, depending on the needs of the individual.
- Knee spaces under countertops should be at least 30 inches wide, 27 inches high, and 19 inches deep.
- While you may have "stepped" countertops, where there are different levels created according to the task, consider how these breaks in continuity will affect the overall efficiency and design, accordingly.

SINKS

- Sinks should be shallow for easy reach—not more than 6 inches deep.
- Find a sink that has the drain toward the rear to keep clear access underneath for knee space.
- A single lever faucet with a pullout sprayer in the nozzle is ideal. A gooseneck design also allows the user to fill tall receptacles.

APPLIANCES

Placement must always be contingent upon how the person may access it with a wheelchair—either parallel or front approach.

- A dishwasher should be next to the sink and ideally at the end of a run so the person may pull up alongside it to reach deep into the racks.
- A conventional stove should be placed where a wheelchair can parallel it. If the space allows, a separate cooktop and wall oven is ideal. The cooktop should have knee space beneath it, and the oven should be mounted at counter height. A glass cooktop is best because it allows pots to be slid in place.
- The best refrigerator design for wheelchair access is a side-by-side type unit. The refrigerator and freezer doors should be able to swing open completely at 180 degrees.

CABINETS

- Base cabinets should have sliding shelves. A Lazy Susan is optimal in a corner cabinet.
- Wall cabinets should be mounted lower than the usual 18 inches above the counter. Instead, mounting them at 15 inches allows access to the higher shelves.

Consider This for a Universal-Design Kitchen

- Wider kitchen entry, at least 32 inches. For kitchens with doors, install an *expandable off-set hinge* to the existing door, which will add 2 inches more of clearance.
- Handles on doors and cabinets should be lever style.
- Use rocker panel light switches as opposed to toggle.
- Nonslip flooring treatment is a must.
- A phone and intercom should be readily accessible.
- Switches and outlets should be installed no higher than 48 inches from the floor.
- Outlets should be no lower than 15 inches from the floor.
- To create a kitchen where both ambulatory and disabled individuals can comfortably use the space, explore the various new technologies that exist in this domain. There are several cabinet and shelf lifts that can automatically be adjusted to the height of the user. As a less high-tech option, consider creating separate work stations to accommodate all users. While this solution may require ample space, smaller kitchens can dedicate one or more work stations to standard heights. It's best to consider all the user's needs and strategize a plan.

Design:

Creating the Ideal Look and Feel for Your Kitchen

Every element in your kitchen will define its look and feel. When dreaming up your perfect kitchen, you need to explore the plethora of exquisite materials, appliances, and fixtures on the market today.

The first thing you should ask yourself is what kind of mood you want your kitchen to create the moment you step foot in it. Do you want fresh and uplifting, country and cozy, playful and kitsch? Once you decide on the mood, keep that feeling in mind as you make your choices.

Where to Get Started

To help choose your kitchen's look and feel try to experience various kitchen designs firsthand. For inspiration browse home and garden shows, go to open houses, and visit kitchen showrooms where you can see various kitchen vignettes set up.

The following are some basic design options that I've categorized to help you define the look and feel you want to create.

Design Options

- **Contemporary**—Today often interchangeable with "modern" and "minimalist," contemporary kitchen designs are sleek, cool, and clean. Squared angles are common, curves are elongated, and structures are reduced to their simplest form.

- **Nature inspired**—A mountain lodge, a serene waterfall, a rain forest—these designs pull from all the wondrous elements nature has to offer and uses many natural resources to do so. Natural stone, bamboo, grasses, and rough-sawn wood are common in these kitchens.

- **Old world**—This design style incorporates beauty from throughout the ages. Be it the sinuous forms of art nouveau, or the peasantlike simplicity of the Italian countryside, old world kitchens can really take you on a mini passage through time from various parts of the world. A less period-intensive perspective of old world crosses into traditional design that draws anywhere from Early American to French country.

- **Transitional**—A marriage of contemporary and traditional, this design offers the best of both worlds. It takes the expected out of traditional and the sterility out of contemporary. Here you can combine fresh and clean with warm and friendly. For example, modern fixtures can be paired with crackled subway tile.

Flooring

The number one question to ask regarding kitchen flooring is if it's impervious to spills. Kitchen floors get wet—whether from a tipped-over glass of juice or a drip coffeemaker that ran amok—you want to be able to get them mopped and cleaned up without any worries.

The next two issues are durability and performance. If you spill red wine, will it stain and ruin the floor? Will it be very slippery when wet?

Last, but not least, style. How will the flooring you choose affect the look and feel of the space? Does it work with the "mood" you want to create?

The following explores some of the more-popular and interesting flooring choices for kitchens. As you browse through them see which best meets these criteria.

Ceramic and Porcelain Tile

A popular choice for kitchens, these tiles are durable, easy to clean, won't absorb water or odors, and are hypoallergenic—they can't harbor mites and allergens. The array of colors, textures, and arrangements are endless. Choosing one may be overwhelming, but the beauty is, whatever you're dreaming up in your head is certain to be out there.

Ceramic tiles are rated by the Porcelain Enamel Institute (PEI). The scale goes from PEI-1 (no-traffic, wall use only) to PEI-5 (the most durable for high-traffic areas).

It's also important to know the difference between ceramic and porcelain tile. The formal distinction can get very technical, but to sum it up, porcelain tiles are generally denser (therefore harder) and more impervious to water than ceramic tiles. Though both tiles are man-made from natural materials, porcelain tiles are fired under higher temperatures, which gives them a higher impervious rating.

The following are some notable characteristics and distinctions between porcelain and ceramic tiles.

Porcelain Tiles

- The clay body or *bisque* of the tile is lighter in color than ceramic tiles.
- They may be marked Porcellanato, which means *porcelain* in Italian.
- Some may be *through-bodied,* which means they're the same color throughout and will have no glaze. This characteristic makes a chip almost unnoticeable.
- They may be glazed or unglazed; unglazed tiles offer more slip resistance.
- They're slightly more expensive than ceramic tiles.
- Because of their high density, they're hard to cut and bond.
- They're extremely well suited for high-traffic areas.

Ceramic Tiles

- The bisque is a dark red terra-cotta color.
- They're typically glazed.
- They cut and bond more easily than porcelain tiles.
- You have the greatest array of choices with ceramic tiles.
- Although less dense than porcelain, some ceramic tiles can offer a PEI-4 rating, which is recommended for all residential applications.

Natural Stone

This genre of flooring includes travertine, marble, granite, slate, and limestone. The exquisiteness of these surfaces is undeniable, and so is the cost. Although it's one of the most-expensive flooring options, its timeless beauty and durability certainly are rewarding. Keep in mind that even though they're durable, they require maintenance. I recommend that stone floors be sealed yearly. They should be cleaned with specialized stone products that won't strip away this seal or damage the surface. Water should not be left to sit, so wiping up after use should be common practice.

Stone can be tumbled, honed, or polished. Tumbled stone offers an imperfect and textured surface. Honed stone is smooth, but has a dull finish. Polished stone is buffed to a high gloss. Each finish offers its own beauty and style, as well as drawbacks to be considered for a kitchen. For example, tumbled stone may feel too rough underfoot and polished stone is extremely slippery when wet.

I'm not a fan of marble in kitchens because of their porous nature. Stains, be them water or oil based, are almost unavoidable and difficult to remove.

Glass Tile

Iridescent, translucent, matte—no matter what the look, glass tiles bring a three-dimensional excitement to a floor that can't go unnoticed. Many glass tiles are made of 100 percent recycled glass, which make them environmentally appealing. Be sure to choose a tile that's suitable for flooring. Do-it-yourselfers should know that cutting glass tile is definitely more finicky than ceramic and is often recommended by the manufacturer to be installed only by a professional with glass tile experience. Glass tile is notably more expensive than ceramic tile, which may make it an ideal accent choice. Be sure to choose one that is PEI rated for flooring.

CONSIDER THIS REGARDING CERAMIC, PORCELAIN, GLASS TILE, AND NATURAL STONE

- It's especially important to consider grout color in a kitchen. A very light-colored grout will inevitably darken unevenly over time. Even if you choose a white tile, use a light gray grout as opposed to white—trust me on this.

- Any *bounce* in the floor (when the subfloor isn't properly secured to joists) will cause the grout to eventually crack and crumble. Be sure that your subfloor is completely stable before considering having one of these floors installed.

- The density and rigidity of these types of flooring make them relentless when it comes to things falling on them. If, say, a glass falls on one, be prepared for it to not only break, but shatter in many pieces. Unfortunately, this holds true for people as well. Kids taking a spill on these floors will likely make any "fall down and go boom" a big "Owey!" Adults with high risk for slip-and-fall accidents are also more vulnerable to injury with these floors.

Hardwood

Some say wood and water don't mix, which would make hardwood floors a no-no for kitchens. But how would that explain wooden boats, canoes, and kayaks? Which got me to thinking. Wood and water do mix as long the wood is properly installed, sealed, and cared for—just like the noble teak of a custom-built sailboat.

Hardwood floors are warm and inviting. What I especially like about hardwood floors is although they're "hard," they're certainly "softer" underfoot than tile or natural stone. If you spend a lot of time working in your kitchen, wood floors are drastically easier on your feet than tile or natural stone. (I've experienced this firsthand at my Mom's house where she has marble floors throughout the kitchen and dining room—after a few days of cooking there for the holidays I had shooting pain up my heels from scurrying around the kitchen barefoot. Yes, I like to cook barefoot.)

Whether they're dark, wide-planked, and distressed or light, narrow-planked and sleek, the following are some considerations that should always be adhered to when choosing and living with a hardwood kitchen floor.

- Only choose a hardwood such as oak, maple, cherry, ash, or walnut. Unlike softwoods (such as spruce, fir, and pine), which more easily absorb ambient moisture, hardwood is resistant to damage and warping.
- Hardwood floors should be properly sealed with a polyurethane or polyacrylic. Penetrating seal and oil finish soaks won't provide enough protection from things like food stains and water spots.
- In very damp climates hardwood is not recommended.
- Spills on wood floors should be wiped up quickly.
- Regular cleaning is crucial to maintain the finish on wood floors.

Laminate

Laminate floors are distinguished by two characteristics—(1) they're floating, not nailed or glued to the subfloor, and (2) the plank face is made to look like a natural surface (say wood or stone), but is in fact a photo rendering atop multiple layers of mixed materials. Laminate floors are durable, affordable, water resistant, and easy to install.

Although many laminate floor manufacturers recommend their product for use in kitchens, they always mention caveats that must be strictly adhered to when installing, such as using a special sealant around the entire perimeter, all expansion spaces, and transitions. The fact is, if water seeps *beneath* the water-resistant surface through a failed seal or joint, the floor *will* buckle. Even if you wipe up the water immediately, if it gets under the surface the damage is done. For this reason, I don't recommend this type of flooring for kitchens that may see a lot of spills.

Engineered Hardwood

Typically, this floor has a top layer of hardwood over several layers of mixed wood and glue—the more layers, the more durable. They may be floating or nailed down like hardwood. In some respects, they are more stable than solid wood, but the same vulnerabilities that apply to laminate floors and hardwood floors also apply to engineered wood. The upside is they're less expensive than hardwood and the floating type are as easy to install as laminate floors.

Bamboo and Cork

Both renewable and sustainable materials, bamboo and cork flooring offer far more than an eco-friendly appeal.

Bamboo floor is 25 percent harder than oak. Because it expands and contracts 50 percent less than hardwood it can be used in high-humidity climates. However, planks could swell if water is left to stand, so wiping them down is a must. Vertical or horizontal grain pattern and natural or carbonized (darker) color offer a modest variety of looks from which to choose.

Cork floors have more benefits and beauty than you could ever imagine. They're naturally stain, moisture, mold, and rot resistant. Although water is okay, flooding the floor is not. Ants and termites want nothing to do with cork so although it's considered a wood, insect infestation is never a concern. It's hard to imagine that a material could be so flexible and durable at the same time, yet it is! It's warm, soft, and anti-skid—perfect for the tootsies. What will surprise you is the expansive variety of colors, patterns, and tile sizes on the market today. Installation is very simple. Maintenance is required, and manufacturers recommend using a finishing/sealant product every 9–12 months.

Vinyl Tile

These tiles are more stylish and durable than ever. Today they are also available oversized and in a wide variety of patterns and colors. They won't gouge, rip, tear from normal household wear, nor indent from heavy appliances or furniture. They're water and stain resistant—perfect for a kitchen. My experience is the glueless type go down and stay down better than the peel-and-stick type. Be sure to purchase ones that are an ⅛-inch thick to ensure greatest durability.

Linoleum

Linoleum flooring has been around for about 150 years. (I remember it on the floor of my grandmother's kitchen. Year after year, holiday after holiday, that floor never showed a shred of age!) Many aspects of this flooring make it an ideal choice for kitchens. It's water and stain resistant, sanitary, and easy to clean and maintain. It's resilience makes it comfortable for standing and reduces shattering from dropped china or glass. True linoleum is made from all natural ingredients—predominately linseed oil from flax plants—but some floors sold under the name "linoleum" are actually made with polyvinyl chloride (PVC). Brands like Forbo Marmoleum are all natural and environmentally friendly—from the materials from which it's made, to manufacturing methods, to biodegradability.

Walls

How much visible wall space is there really in your kitchen? It's likely that cabinets and the refrigerator will occupy much of the wall space. For this reason, it's important to make what you do see of your walls really count.

Before deciding on a wall material, finish, or color I ask myself what is the intended purpose of the walls in this space (other than holding up the ceiling!). Do I want them to act as a neutral backdrop for bold fixtures and cabinets? Do I want the color of the walls to set the overall mood of the room? Do I want a border tile to unite the entire space?

Ask yourself questions such as these to help make your decisions, and don't be afraid to be adventurous.

Design Options

- **Paint** has limitless options in color and design. Painting techniques such as faux finishes and glazing will bring added visual interest to a bare wall. High-contrast color molding creates dimension in the space. A stencil or trompe l'oeil can be used to accent an interesting architectural feature like around a vaulted window.

  Know that kitchens are hard on walls. Especially if you have a high-traffic kitchen, be sure to choose a paint that is formulated to be washable and resistant to moisture and mildew. Generally, a paint that has a smooth and shinier surface is less able to hold in moisture and grime and performs better in busy kitchens.

- **Wainscott and beadboard panels** range from simple to stately. They can make a kitchen seem like it's part of a beach cottage or a turn-of-the-century mansion. They can run floor to ceiling, or to or below chair rail height (approximately one-third of the wall height)—either horizontally or vertically. I've also seen them used up through the backsplash—of which I'm not really a fan. Splatters on beadboard are not easily wiped away because of the grooves in the wood.

- **Tiled walls** in kitchens are an old-meets-new design option. In the early 20th century subway-tiled walls were common in kitchens. More recently tiled walls, especially subway tile, have become very popular in kitchens. I especially like them in kitchens because they are so durable and are easily wiped clean. If tile throughout the space is not desirable because of budget or design taste, another option is to tile just one wall of the kitchen.

- **Wallpaper and wallpaper border** are a quick and inexpensive way to perk up a kitchen. Long gone are the days where the "paper" and starchy glue gave safe haven and feeding ground for bugs. Solid vinyl wallpapers are washable and scrubbable—absolute must-have features for kitchens.

Cabinetry

For me nothing screams opulence like custom cabinetry. There are so many aspects of cabinetry to consider. Be prepared to spend an inordinate amount of time making your choices, and rightly so. Cabinetry can end up being the most costly aspect of your kitchen as well as provide the biggest impact.

Design Options

Here are some basic cabinetry features and topics you'll need to consider.

- **Layout**—What will work best in that particular space given its dimensions and who will be using it? If there's ever a time to work with a professional designer, now would be it.

- **Wood characteristics**—Every wood has its own signature, and of course price. For example, maple is characterized by its smooth even grain, whereas pecan is known for its dramatic color variations. Walnut runs about twice the price of, say, white oak.

- **Finish**—Stains will enhance the wood grain, opaques provide a solid-body color, and glazes will highlight deep crevices or all visible cabinet parts. Distressed techniques provide a vintage warmth and charm. No matter what the finish, it must be able to protect the wood and wipe up easy with a damp cloth.

- **Door styles and pulls**—Proportions, shapes, and details all need to be considered especially since doors and pulls are such a prominent part of the look of the cabinets.

- **Quality**—Cabinets should be of solid-wood construction and hardwood framed. Hardware, guides, and joints should all be top quality. Smooth operation of drawers is a must. Check if the manufacturer offers a limited lifetime warranty.

Countertops

Countertops see a lot of action in a kitchen. Visually, they have a huge impact on the look of your space. Because they serve both a design element and work surface it's important to do your homework before choosing one (or more than one, if so desired). There are two common mistakes people make when choosing a countertop: clashing color or pattern with the floor or cabinets and choosing a material or color that either doesn't wear well, or is more trouble to maintain than they had anticipated.

I like the idea of applying various countertop materials as dictated by use and design of the space. For example, using butcher-block top only next to a second sink for cleaning and chopping vegetables. Or, say you have a peninsula that serves as an eating area and gives way to a den, you may choose a different, more formal countertop for it than in the rest of the kitchen.

Design Options

The following are some countertop options to consider. Note that glass tiles are not recommended for kitchen countertops because they scratch easy and may require large grout lines. They should be considered for accents and backsplashes instead.

- **Ceramic and porcelain** tile countertops can offer a wide variety of looks because of the plethora of types and colors. They are highly durable, and stain and heat resistant. A drawback may be the grout lines—when wiping down the surface these nooks and crannies can trap food particles. Also, if not properly sealed, grout can stain.

- **Granite** is considered by many to be the ultimate in countertop surface—both aesthetically and functionally. It's one of the hardest materials nature offers, making it highly scratch and crack resistant. Hot pans can go right on them straight from the oven. Their smooth surface is also ideal for rolling and kneading. Unlike marble, it's stain resistant, and wipes down with ease. Granite carries a look of luxury and is always considered an upgrade in a kitchen.

- **Soapstone, marble, travertine, and limestone** are all quarried stone that offer unique and natural beauty to countertops. As compared to granite, however, they are inferior with regard to durability. They are far more porous and less dense, making them more prone to stains and scratches. It is imperative that they are maintained with a proper sealer.

- **Engineered stone** combines the durability of natural stone with the flexibility and variety of man-made surfaces. Made predominately of crushed quartz this material is highly heat, stain, and scratch resistant. Considered an advantage over natural stone is its consistency in pigment and pattern. Costwise, it's about the same price as granite.

- **Solid surface** countertops are 100 percent man-made material. They can be molded with a built-in backsplash and offer a variety of edging and borders with no visible seams, giving a fluid look to countertops. Textures, colors, and finishes are abundant. As the name implies, being solid throughout, there is no veneer that can chip and scratches can be buffed away. Although they are made to be stain and heat resistant, they are not as durable as natural stone. Scorching and staining will occur in certain conditions.

- **Laminate** countertops are one of the more-affordable surfaces. In addition to being sensibly priced you can relish in the vast number of looks, patterns, and colors to choose from. It's important to choose one that is high quality to ensure wear resistance. Chipping and scratching are the biggest drawbacks of these surfaces.

- **Concrete** is a unique and diverse material that offers a natural look to countertops. It can be cast to fit almost any shape your kitchen calls for. Various stains and finishes can make it look and feel like quarried stone. In its natural state, concrete is porous, but sealers are applied making them water and stain resistant. While concrete is impervious to heat and scratches, the sealer is not. Placing hot objects and cutting on the surface will compromise the sealer, therefore resulting in damage to the concrete.

- **Stainless steel** is ideal for an industrial or contemporary look for a kitchen. They offer sleek and seamless design. While they can't be cut on, they are highly durable with respect to heat and staining. Of all the surfaces, they are most easily kept sanitary. Something to consider is the noisy aspect of the surface—be prepared for "clinking and clanking" as you work on this surface.

- **Wood and bamboo** countertops offer a natural appeal to the look of a kitchen. Bamboo has gained popularity because of its renewable and environmentally friendly properties. These surfaces are not one solid piece of wood, but rather many pieces glued together. For this reason the various grains that will be visible change the top's look—namely face grain, end grain, and edge grain. These surfaces are known for their excellent properties for cutting and chopping. You must carefully consider what type of finish is applied to the wood since it will impact the wood's ability to be water, stain, and scratch resistant. Use of either of these materials in areas that are perpetually wet is not recommended.

- **Recycled materials** such as paper, plastic, stone, and glass are being used to create innovative countertop surfaces. They come in a wide variety of looks and colors. Each offers environmentally friendly and healthy properties, but no countertop material has zero impact on the planet.

Appliances, Sinks, and Faucets

These elements are the real nuts and bolts of a kitchen. Every one of them is used hands-on every day—turned, pulled, opened, closed, drained, and so on. Whatever your design choice, be sure that they're durable, high quality, and installed properly.

Design Options

There are several ways to go about choosing appliances, sinks, and faucets. Here are a couple of methods to help guide you through your quest.

- **Browse manufacturers' suites, collections, and ensembles.** For example, matching stovetop, wall oven, and refrigerator. Because everything is based around a common design, the guesswork is taken out of the equation. All you have to do is find a collection, color, and finish that fulfill your dream kitchen.

- **Choose pieces individually.** Where nothing "matches," but the pieces work together harmoniously. This method of choosing articles is a real kitchen-person's approach because it gives you the opportunity to choose the best of the best, no matter who the manufacturer.

- **Be mindful of the intended purpose.** Yes, you've fallen in love with the design and concept of the AGA English Cooker (the one that's on and hot all the time), but are you prepared for the additional heat it adds to the room temperature? You've decided that stainless is the look you crave but will the perpetual smudges and fingertips on your stainless-steel appliances annoy you? Style and innovation are certainly alluring, but not at the cost of functionality and purpose.

Tips on Appliances

STOVE

- Gas or electric? Gas is preferred by chefs because the temperature on the burner is more readily controlled. Dual-fuel models exist where burners are gas, and the oven is electric. If gas is not available in your area you may consider installing a propane tank if cooking with fire is what you desire.

- A well-insulated oven is crucial for energy efficiency. It will also keep the kitchen cooler and will be safer to the touch, especially if children are around.

- Separate cooktop and wall oven offer a custom look and added convenience of two separate cooking stations. It will, however, reduce counter workspace and is almost twice as costly as a freestanding range.

- Combo wall ovens with built-in microwaves are great space-savers. However, check the unit's performance history. I've seen many where the microwave goes before the oven.

- Glass tops are certainly sleek in design, but be aware that special cleaners are necessary to keep them looking good.

- "Full motion" grates over burners allow you to shift pots from burners without having to lift them.

REFRIGERATOR

- Because we spend seven times as much time in the fridge as opposed to the freezer, having the fridge at eye level has regained popularity. FYI, "bottom mount" indicates freezer on the bottom and "top mount" is freezer on top.

- Look for a bottom mount with drawers that pull out and tilt for easier access.

- Look for units that have the ice dispenser basket built in the door, which is space-saving.

- Adjustable shelves and specialized bottle-and-can compartments are space-saving and offer immense convenience.

- Essentially this appliance runs all the time. Finding one that is Energy Star qualified will use less energy and save you money to run it yearly.

DISHWASHER

- Check how many levels and directions of sprayers there are. Typically, the more there are, the cleaner the dishes.

- A dishwasher with a built-in grinder will save you water and time with no need for prerinsing.

- Check if the unit has "sound insulation" if a noisy dishwasher will be disruptive to you.

- A dishwasher that doesn't fit your dishes or glassware properly won't make you happy no matter how great it is. If you know you have, say, very tall glasses or oversized plates, bring them for a test-fit when shopping for a unit.

- Energy Star–qualified units will use less energy and save you money to run yearly. Additionally, check to see how many gallons of water it uses for a load. High-efficiency units will clean effectively using considerably less water than other units, saving you money on your water bill.

Tips on Sinks

- If choosing a stainless-steel sink, know that there are various grades and gauges to consider. Gauge measures thickness where the lower the gauge, the thicker the steel. Substantial thickness is important to avoid bows and dings, as well as noisy clinking and clanking; 18 or 20 gauge is considered a good choice for residential use. Premium-grade steel is crucial to avoid corrosion and increase durability. "Type 302" is considered best for residential sinks.

- Undermounted sinks (as opposed to drop-ins) make wiping down the countertop easier because there's no rim on the counter that will trap water and particles.

- Apron front sinks are easier on your back because they bring the sink several inches closer to you than standard ones.

- There are good-quality porcelain enamel sinks bonded to an enameling grade metal that are lighter, less expensive, and easier to install than cast iron sinks. However, be aware that they may be more prone to chipping and scorching.

- If space allows, a double or triple bowl sink allows simultaneous uses. For example, you can soak pots and wash vegetables at the same time. If possible, a small second sink will free up the main one and create an additional workstation. The plumbing rough-in for this fixture should be considered at the design stages.

- Often, the drain strainer will not be included with the sink and will need to be purchased individually. Be sure to purchase one that matches and fits the sink.

Tips on Faucets

- A single-handle faucet is very easy to operate because temperature and pressure are controlled with one movement. Even more convenient are faucets with foot controls. After only being used in medical settings, today they are available for residential use. They avoid you having to touch the handles with hands that may be contaminated from raw foods like poultry, making them extremely hygienic.

- Be sure to purchase a faucet with a spout that swivels and has a reach that's long enough to service the sink bowl(s). It should also be arched to accommodate tall pitchers and pots.

- Faucets with a spout that's a pull-out sprayer are very handy, and don't require an additional hole in the sink or countertop deck.

- "Washerless" operation refers to cartridge, ball, and ceramic disk-type faucets. They don't require a washer to create a seal (as do compression-type faucets) and tend to be less prone to leaks and require maintenance.

- Consider a pot-filler faucet installed by the stove to take the burden out of filling and moving large, heavy pots of water from the sink to the stove. The plumbing rough-in for this fixture should be considered at the design stages.

Lighting

It's important to have a well-lit kitchen. A large overhead fixture is important to illuminate the entire space. Unfortunately with just one overhead light you're likely to end up working in your own shadow—making adequate task lighting crucial for work stations. There may be occasions where simply accent or "mood" lighting is all you'll want to enjoy a cup of coffee or chat with friends. The following will explore the various types of lighting—overhead, task, and accent—all of which are necessary to create ideal lighting scenarios in your kitchen.

Overhead

A well-illuminating overhead fixture is needed for general lighting purposes. Personally, I'm not a fan of a single overhead light source, especially fluorescents. Unfortunately, many kitchens are designed with this type of light setup. Fluorescents are greener and more cost efficient than incandescent bulbs, but cast an unappealing light color. Happily, there are a vast array of eco-friendly bulbs such as compact fluorescents (CFLs) and light-emitting-diodes (LEDs) that have recently improved their quality of light and are more pleasing on the eye. Consider some of these more aesthetically pleasing overhead choices for your kitchen.

- **Recessed**—Also referred to as cans, these are an ideal choice for medium to large kitchens. Lights can be strategically spaced out over the entire room. They work very well on dimmers, which allow you to control the amount of light depending on your mood or the time of day.

- **Track lighting**—There are many versions of track lighting, but their common attribute is their ability to be configured specifically to fit the space.

- **Chandeliers**—Hanging fixtures offer a sense of drama and style. I especially like to supplement one large overhead chandelier with matching smaller ones (pendant) that can hang over, say, an island.

- **Flush mounted**—These are fine for a small kitchen, but will not suffice in medium and large ones. Some of these fixtures have sockets that are directional and can be pivoted to aim the light as desired.

Task

No doubt crucial in a kitchen, proper task lighting makes all the difference when it comes to working comfortably over workstations. Task lighting can be created in several ways using track, recessed, spot, and undercabinet lights. Undercabinet lights can be thin fluorescents, low-voltage linear, or puck lights, which may be surface or flush mounted. In this application, I especially like Xenon bulbs because they produce a brighter light than fluorescents, run cooler than halogens, and are extremely energy efficient. With regard to track, recessed, and spot lights it's imperative that they be properly positioned over the work area. For example, a recessed light over the sink should be, well, over the sink and not end up over your head, which will cast a shadow.

Accent

Accent lighting adds dimension to your kitchen. Spot lights can be use to highlight cabinetry. Two wall sconces can flank an eating area. A small shaded lamp can offer warmth and charm when set on an open-faced cabinet shelf. Although intended to complement overhead lighting, accent lights are a must to create an inviting look and feel. Task lights can also act as accent lighting given their placement—like under cabinets.

Index

Wiley Publishing, Inc. End-User License Agreement

5. **Remedies.**

   (a) WPI's entire liability and your exclusive remedy for defects in materials and workmanship shall be limited to replacement of the Media, which may be returned to WPI with a copy of your receipt at the following address: Software Media Fulfillment Department, Attn.: *Norma Vally's Kitchen Fix-ups*, Wiley Publishing, Inc., 10475 Crosspoint Blvd., Indianapolis, IN 46256, or call (800) 762-2974. Please allow four to six weeks for delivery. This Limited Warranty is void if failure of the Media has resulted from accident, abuse, or misapplication. Any replacement Media will be warranted for the remainder of the original warranty period or thirty (30) days, whichever is longer.

   (b) In no event shall WPI or the author be liable for any damages whatsoever (including without limitation damages for loss of business profits, business interruption, loss of business information, or any other pecuniary loss) arising from the use of or inability to use the Book or the Media, even if WPI has been advised of the possibility of such damages.

   (c) Because some jurisdictions do not allow the exclusion or limitation of liability for consequential or incidental damages, the above limitation or exclusion may not apply to you.

6. **U.S. Government Restricted Rights.** Use, duplication, or disclosure of the Media for or on behalf of the United States of America, its agencies and/or instrumentalities "U.S. Government" is subject to restrictions as stated in paragraph (c)(1)(ii) of the Rights in Technical Data and Computer Software clause of DFARS 252.227-7013, or subparagraphs (c) (1) and (2) of the Commercial Computer Software - Restricted Rights clause at FAR 52.227-19, and in similar clauses in the NASA FAR supplement, as applicable.

7. **General.** This Agreement constitutes the entire understanding of the parties and revokes and supersedes all prior agreements, oral or written, between them and may not be modified or amended except in a writing signed by both parties hereto that specifically refers to this Agreement. This Agreement shall take precedence over any other documents that may be in conflict herewith. If any one or more provisions contained in this Agreement are held by any court or tribunal to be invalid, illegal, or otherwise unenforceable, each and every other provision shall remain in full force and effect.